Easy Homeopathy

Also by Edward Shalts, M.D., D.Ht.

The American Institute of Homeopathy Handbook for Parents

Easy Homeopathy

The 7 Essential Remedies
You Need for Common
Illnesses and First Aid

EDWARD SHALTS, M.D., D.Ht.

VICE PRESIDENT, NATIONAL CENTER FOR HOMEOPATHY

WITH STEPHANIE GUNNING

McGraw-Hill

New York   Chicago   San Francisco   Lisbon   London   Madrid   Mexico City
Milan   New Delhi   San Juan   Seoul   Singapore   Sydney   Toronto

Library of Congress Cataloging-in-Publication Data

Shalts, Edward, 1955–
    Easy homeopathy : the 7 essential remedies you need for common illnesses and first aid /
Edward Shalts, with Stephanie Gunning.
       p.   cm.
    Includes bibliographical references and index.
    ISBN 0-07-145758-5 (book : alk. paper)
    1. Homeopathy—Popular works.   I. Gunning, Stephanie, 1958–   II. Title.

RX601.S52   2005
615.5′32—dc22   2005027194

ISBN 0-07-145758-5

Interior design by Monica Baziuk

McGraw-Hill books are available at special quantity discounts to use as premiums and sales
promotions, or for use in corporate training programs. For more information, please write to the
Director of Special Sales, Professional Publishing, McGraw-Hill, Two Penn Plaza, New York, NY
10121-2298. Or contact your local bookstore.

The information contained in this book is intended to provide helpful and informative material on
the subject addressed. It is not intended to serve as a replacement for professional medical advice.
Any use of the information in this book is at the reader's discretion. The author and publisher
specifically disclaim any and all liability arising directly or indirectly from the use or application of
any information contained in this book. A health-care professional should be consulted regarding
your specific situation. All case studies herein are based on composites of real case studies, and
they are intended to provide general information rather than to represent real individuals or specific
situations.

This book is printed on acid-free paper.

To my beloved wife, Natasha, who provides me with continuous encouragement and tremendous support

Contents

PART 1

Getting Started in Homeopathy

PART 2

The Seven Remedies That Should Be in Every Medicine Cabinet

PART 3

Helpful Hints and Easy Solutions

Acknowledgments

FIRST, I'D LIKE to acknowledge the godmother of this book, Rona Lichtenberg. I would like to thank literary agent Stephany Evans for providing me with indispensable guidance and assistance. I am also grateful to editor Michele Matrisciani, project editor Charles Fisher, copyeditor Laura Gabler, and others at McGraw-Hill for their ongoing support and faith in this project. The book would not speak to the reader as clearly as it does without the invaluable help of my coauthor, Stephanie Gunning.

This book grew on the shoulders of many other excellent books written by remarkable people. Just to name a few, I'd like to thank George Vithoulkas, Paul Herscu, Amy Rothenberg, and Roger Morrison for their brilliant texts and teaching in the field of homeopathy. In the preparation of this book, I read most of the popular homeopathic literature published in the English language since 1980. I thank the authors of all these books for the lessons I learned from them. I would like to thank my patients who, without knowing it, taught me important lessons about homeopathy.

In addition, I extend my deepest gratitude to Drs. Woodson Merrell, Robert Schiller, Benjamin Kligler, and Roberta Lee for opening new horizons and providing me with continuous encouragement and advice. It is also my great pleasure to recognize the tremendous support provided to me by Barbara Glickstein.

The list of people who were instrumental in the successful production of this book would not be complete without mentioning my wife, Natasha, and my parents, Emma and Boris. They have constantly pushed me to higher standards and encouraged all my efforts in the difficult field of homeopathy. Lately, Boris has been doing it from far away. I hope at least some information can still reach his soul wherever he is. One also should not underestimate the important role of children in their parents' lives. My daughters, Dora and Polina, have always provided a friendly, loving atmosphere and served as willing participants in the homeopathic miracles in our house.

Introduction
Why Homeopathy?

HOMEOPATHIC REMEDIES BELONG on the shelf in your home medicine cabinet alongside your aspirin, hydrogen peroxide, adhesive tape, and sterile gauze bandages. Without needing to become an expert in the field, you can build a first-aid kit of basic remedies that have the potential to dramatically improve the quality of your daily life. The purpose of *Easy Homeopathy* is to reveal the brilliance of homeopathy: one remedy can work for many different ailments.

Homeopathy can be used to treat a wide range of everyday ailments. When you match the correct remedy to a set of symptoms, it quickly resolves many issues. It cuts short the duration of symptoms, which often begin to dissipate almost immediately—perhaps in as few as fifteen to twenty minutes. But it doesn't mask problems. Homeopaths don't view symptoms as foes, merely as noticeable responses. When I cut an onion, for instance, I cry because its vapors irritate my eyes. To *alarm* me, my eyes itch. To *protect* me, my body releases tears that wash the vapors away. Homeopathy is an intervention that helps the body naturally respond better to whatever it faces.

Since homeopathy can catch and disrupt illness at the onset, it helps prevent relatively benign conditions from evolving into more dangerous ones. Furthermore, unlike conventional drugs, which have the potential to produce unpleasant side effects, homeopathic remedies are exceedingly safe. Because they contain highly diluted natural substances, you can take a dose or two without worrying about harming yourself. They tend to produce either a rapid and favorable result or no result whatsoever.

All these qualities make homeopathy an ideal home-aid tool.

Imagine that a normally healthy child comes to his parents' bed in the middle of the night, frightened and with a high fever. His face is red, his head is hot, his hands are cold, and his pupils are enlarged. A typical way that concerned parents would handle an alarming incident like this is to give their child fever medication. Although a drug could provide him temporary relief by reducing fever, it might mask a potentially serious problem. On the other hand, if the child's parents instead give him homeopathic *Belladonna* 30C, he most probably will go to sleep within fifteen minutes, his fever will break on its own, and in the morning he'll feel fine. And should the *Belladonna* fail to do the trick within half an hour, the parents can always seek professional help. Homeopathy either will resolve the situation completely or it won't do anything. It's perfectly safe, and it doesn't limit your options.

As both a medical doctor and a practicing homeopath, I am continually amazed at how well homeopathy works in acute situations where conventional medicine has little to offer. Moreover, there are certain conditions—such as teething pain, infant colic, poison ivy, grief, and the early stages of colds and influenza—for which conventional medicine has found no solution. Homeopathy offers specific and highly effective cures for these and similar conditions. The approach is based on an entirely different model of health care than allopathic medicine, an approach geared toward healing the whole person versus temporary suppression of unpleasant symptoms.

While it would be ineffective, for instance, to give an antidepressant to someone for any condition other than an emotional one, it is conceivable in homeopathy to use the exact same remedy to treat both an emotional problem (such as grief) and a physical problem (such as cold sores). In acute cases there are always components that express themselves physically and components that express themselves emotionally. These differ according to the individual who has the problem. Conventional medicine doesn't usually consider the emotions in the process of finding a medication for a physical ailment. But when you are selecting a homeopathic remedy, you look for patterns that are characteristic for a particular person and describe the whole person. That's why one person with a high fever who is also scared and restless may need *Aconitum* for a head cold while another person with a head cold and fever who looks drugged may need *Belladonna*.

If I succeed at nothing else in this book, I hope to persuade you that making a choice to try homeopathy is not an either-or proposition. Rather it is an either-*and* proposition. It allows us to reserve our most powerful weapons, such as painkillers, hormones, and antibiotics, for drastic situations. It protects against complications of medications and other conventional treatments, like chemotherapy, radiation, and surgery. In addition, homeopathy can often reduce the dosage of medication required to manage some chronic diseases or can eliminate the need for medication altogether.

Contrary to popular belief (or at least the belief of skeptics), there is no inherent conflict of interest between using conventional medicine and homeopathy. It does not delay you from seeking medical attention. A homeopathic remedy can be taken—or given to a child—at home while you are placing a phone call to the doctor or in the car or an ambulance on the way to the emergency room. Like other respected forms of first aid, it can lessen the severity of the trauma or symptoms for which you are seeking care. If the homeopathic remedy you or your loved ones take succeeds in alleviating the pain and discomfort, it's a safe bet that everyone involved will be glad—including the doctor. It is not unusual for homeopathy to produce rapid results.

At the Continuum Center for Health and Healing, where I used to work, I supervised medical fellows and asked them to run cases by me if they needed help. On a summer's afternoon a few years ago, one of these young doctors told me she had a three-year-old boy in her office who was in distress after having been stung on his foot by a large insect the day before. Overnight his foot had become painfully swollen, hot, and red, and now the swelling and redness were spreading up his leg. Because she was concerned that gangrene might set in, the doctor planned to give him antibiotics. But I persuaded her to explore an alternative. Perhaps homeopathy could provide a less intrusive solution.

The boy's mother agreed to let me examine her son. Among other things, she informed me that the bite had made him extremely irritable. Considering the key physical and emotional indications, I immediately thought to use the remedy *Apis* 30C, made from the honeybee. I gave him a single tablet diluted in a glass of water, a very tiny amount. Then we waited for only twenty minutes. At that point, both the doctor and the mother could discern that the redness on the boy's leg and foot was fading and the swelling had gone down. He was significantly calmer. The *Apis* was clearly working.

In order to ensure the boy's safety, the doctor gave the mother a prescription for antibiotics—just in case—and asked her to check in that night by phone. But the boy never needed the medication. By the next morning, he was much better. When he was brought back to the office two days later for a follow-up exam, no evidence of a problem remained.

Another remarkable case resulted after I had been treating a man for severe depression and several other chronic complaints for a period of months. Everything had improved except one thing—he still got terrible migraine headaches quite frequently. Beforehand he would experience visual distortions. During the headaches he'd feel severely nauseous and vomit profusely. I suggested that the man take *Iris* 30C the next time he sensed a headache coming on. He did. As a result of taking it that one time, he hasn't had another headache for several years.

This case shows you that homeopathy—when it's indicated—can dramatically change someone's life. Based on my knowledge of the remedy and the man's history, I was able to pinpoint the remedy *Iris*. Realistically, however, it won't cure everyone who experiences migraines—only people with a similar constellation of indicators. Still, the relief this man gained is the kind of remarkable improvement that homeopathy is regularly known to promote.

Here's another example of homeopathy saving the day. My daughter got her finger slammed in a car door one time and was in terrible, unbelievable pain. With a quick check, I determined that her skin and bones had not been broken. If they had been, I would have taken her to the hospital immediately. Since they weren't, I gave her three pellets of *Hypericum* 30C. Her pain was reduced by 50 percent in thirty minutes. Because the trauma was so severe, I then gave her a second dose of the same remedy. By the end of the day there were no symptoms—no bruising, no swelling—whatsoever.

After more than twenty years of practice, I have come in contact with thousands of individuals of different ages in every imaginable state of health. To the best of my ability, I always treat my patients as if they were family, and my family members are treated almost exclusively by homeopathy. By birth I am Russian, by choice American. In my native tongue, the word for family, *semja* (pronounced sem-yah), literally means "seven of me." Therefore, I have chosen to center this book on the seven remedies that I find most life transforming and most frequently useful: *Aconitum, Arnica, Belladonna, Chamomilla, Gelsemium, Ignatia,* and *Nux vomica*.

Several dozen additional remedies—including *Apis, Iris,* and *Hypericum*, mentioned earlier—are featured because they grow in importance upon occasion, like a pawn on a chessboard that graduates to being a queen. Having awareness of their availability and making sure there's a supply on hand prior to going through one of these specific scenarios (for example, getting an insect bite or feeling seasick) may prove a godsend.

We live in an increasingly health-conscious society, where the benefits of preventive steps like taking vitamin supplements, getting regular exercise, and eating organic produce are well understood. These are measures that increase our resilience. In the modern world, where alternative and conventional medicine now offer us so many choices, homeopathy has an important role to play as a first line of defense. It can help you gain more control over your health and to be independent of drugs.

Unfortunately, in our culture today we have also learned to rely too heavily on medications like painkillers, sleeping pills, antihistamines, antibiotics, and antacids for a variety of everyday ailments. These drugs are now so common that most of us—physicians and consumers alike—scarcely think of them as powerful, heroic, or radical.

Have you ever heard the old expression "Don't use a cannon to kill a fly"? There is no question that drugs can be highly effective in alleviating our immediate symptoms, such as headache, insomnia, the sneezes and sniffles of allergies, indigestion, and so on. But the success of powerful medications comes with a heavy price tag. A steady influx of drugs apparently weakens our defenses, making us more and more dependent on help from the outside.

Homeopathic medicine offers us an opportunity to regain control of our health. Its approach to wellness emphasizes the body's innate capacity for self-healing and self-restoration. Rather than suppressing symptoms, as medications generally do, it expands the body's innate capacity to fight illness. In numerous scenarios homeopathy can bring us the same kind of relief that we seek from conventional medicine, while strengthening our body so that it can successfully resist illness in the future.

PART

1

GETTING STARTED
IN HOMEOPATHY

🌿 1 🌿

Is It Healthy to Be Sick?

Do not swat a fly on your friend's head with a hatchet.

—Confucius

YOU AND YOUR FAMILY deserve to have access to the best health care available—care that is noninvasive, produces no negative side effects, and doesn't cost an arm and a leg in the bargain. That's why *Easy Homeopathy* exists. The seven primary homeopathic remedies in this book, and their few dozen secondary counterparts, form the basis of a first-aid protocol that you can rapidly learn to use to effectively complement your conventional medical care. When they are appropriately applied, these homeopathic remedies can swiftly relieve discomfort so you and your loved ones may get on with the important daily matters of living. After all, good health is the foundation of everything we do in our lives.

You picked up this book because you're interested in learning more about homeopathy, an intervention that helps the body naturally respond better to whatever physical, emotional, and mental challenges it faces. *Easy Homeopathy* covers sudden, short-term

3

problems. Homeopathy has been proven effective in the treatment of acute ailments, such as the common cold, diarrhea, and earache, as well as in the treatment of chronic diseases, such as allergies and panic disorder. Before you will be ready to put homeopathy to practical use, there are a few important concepts you need to understand, starting with the nature of homeopathic remedies and how they can serve you.

What Are Homeopathic Remedies?

Homeopathy is a medical specialty that uses diluted natural substances known as remedies to stimulate the body's innate capacity for healing. These remedies have been both diluted and shaken multiple times in order to give them potency. Oddly, the more times remedies are diluted and shaken—in other words, the less concentrated they are—the stronger they become. And substances that are diluted without being shaken do not produce the same healing effects in those who consume them as the ones that have been shaken. No one knows exactly why this is true, even though it is what the clinical and laboratory research has confirmed.

Why are diluted substances used to make homeopathic remedies? According to the principle that like cures like, which is the foundation of homeopathy, any substance that causes a combination of symptoms in a healthy, sensitive individual can cure similar symptoms in the sick. Essentially, homeopathy gives us a nonharmful way to sample a "poison." Remedies are so thoroughly diluted that we can barely detect the raw material.

Homeopathy was discovered more than two hundred years ago by Samuel Hahnemann, a prominent German physician, chemist, and pharmacologist. Since then, homeopathic remedies have proven enormously successful in providing individualized help and highly effective cures for many illnesses without causing any side effects or complications. They are also easy to use, because each remedy is prescribed only to cure a unique constellation of symptoms—a picture, if you will. When the patient and the remedy share an identical picture, you give the remedy to the patient. If they don't, you make a different choice. Choosing a remedy for an acute condition is relatively straightforward, because acute conditions tend to present clear, easy-to-see symptoms.

Perhaps the most difficult concept to grasp about homeopathy, albeit the one that makes it so incredibly powerful, is that at any given moment there is only one special remedy a person would benefit from taking. Whenever you can identify this correct remedy, it initiates a cascade of healing throughout the recipient's entire integrated being. A single remedy can improve that person's physical, emotional, and mental well-being.

A Few of the Reasons That Homeopathy Is More Important Today than Ever Before

After we are born, our bodies need training in order to learn what to do and then, later, to upgrade to proficiency. Just think about it. It takes children a while to learn how to walk without falling down and to speak in full sentences. Developing these skills involves frequent stimulation from their parents and other adults. Isolated children fail to acquire intellectual skills that are even close to those of normal toddlers. Similarly, the immune system needs training. In order to remain healthy, it must be able to differentiate between life-forms that are its "friends" and its "enemies." Children who've been given the chance to encounter different germs are more proficient at averting disease.

A backyard in the country and a sandbox in the city are excellent training grounds for the immune system. In these environments, children touch different objects, including the soil, plants, worms, other children, and so forth, exposing them to various microbes—bacteria and viruses (aka bugs). The immune system fights back, often winning right away and growing stronger as a result. Other times an infection occurs. The immune system learns from that experience, too. A fever speeds up the production of immune cells and creates an unfriendly environment in the body for the bugs. A bunch of other symptoms also develop that indicate the body is undergoing a healing process. If sick children are kept home for a few days so the immune system has enough time and acceptable conditions to get over the aggression, it becomes smarter, more capable.

A cold? Yes! Bring it on! Time to have a training fight! That's the attitude I would like to see more parents adopt. But this rarely occurs anymore. Nowadays there's an active exchange of viruses between exhausted schoolchildren who, after receiving doses of fever medication and decongestants, were sent to class by parents. This exchange is unrestricted by natural defense mechanisms. Rather than fighting bugs naturally, most kids don't get the rest they need and aren't allowed to experience the healing mechanisms of their symptoms. Powerful medications (often unnecessary) prevent them from having a fever to speed up the immune response and having nasal discharges that flush their bodies out. If modern families reversed the cultural tendency to suppress symptoms and let children be a little sick from time to time, we would be a much healthier society.

Does this advice seem primitive to you? Perhaps. But there's scientific evidence that it is reliable advice. As it turns out, many children in developing countries still live much as children in the industrialized nations did in the 1950s. Interestingly, although these children often suffer from diseases related to poverty and poor hygiene, they have significantly fewer chronic illnesses, like allergies. In simple terms, allergic reactions are the result of an uneducated immune system that doesn't know what to do. By overreacting to natural substances, like pollen, that normally wouldn't be perceived as an enemy, the immune system turns against the body it's supposed to protect.

At the beginning of the chapter, I cited a quote from Confucius: "Do not swat a fly on your friend's head with a hatchet." You're probably wondering, "What's the big deal? That's so obvious!" Well, not really. You see, in Western medicine people typically take a shock-and-awe approach to disease, with an emphasis on wiping out symptoms rather than viewing symptoms as signs of the healing process.

Parents blame physicians for overprescribing medications. Physicians respond that frequently they are driven by a wish of parents to do everything possible to protect children from infections and complications. The same situation is true for adults. I can't even begin to tell you how often patients walk into my office and say, "Doctor, I need an antidepressant," or, "Doc, I am studying for a difficult test. Give me a prescription for a stimulant" (though they actually name a drug).

Who is in the right and who is in the wrong here? As always, the answer lies right smack in the middle. We, parents and doctors alike, grew up in a culture of fear, constantly feeling as if we were in a medical emergency. Pain? Take painkillers! Fever? Suppress it! Where did this attitude come from? Obviously, there are many possible explanations. The most obvious is the history of medicine in the twentieth century.

Proprietary medications—drugs that are patented and earn companies revenue—first appeared on the market after successful trials that took place during World War I. Being able to respond immediately to potentially disabling problems was critical to the success of the army. If there was a wound or pain, they wanted immediate removal of the pain and suffering. "Stitch 'em up, and send 'em back to the battlefield." Another major development was the industrial revolution. Businesses adopted a militaristic sense of urgency. Thousands of people had to get to work every day. Like foot soldiers, they had to get better immediately, no matter what. Missing work was a disaster to be prevented by heroic measures.

A false feeling of omnipotence was also born in Western culture as a result of our great technological advances. We believed that the human body was similar to a machine and interventions would keep it running efficiently. These two concepts—urgent care and the sense that we knew almost everything—drove medicine and our mentality for more than a century. Certainly it was a self-fulfilling prophecy. Vaccinations eliminated deadly infections, sophisticated anesthesia and painkillers diminished pain, antibiotics killed germs, and powerful psychotropic medications seemed to make psychiatric patients so much better. We bought into it.

Today people go on the Internet to do research so they can ask their doctors the right questions. The impulse is pure, and there's also an inherent watchfulness. Doctors are aware of third parties, including lawyers, insurance companies, bureaucrats, and the media, who are looking over their shoulders all the time to ensure they'll do what is safe and correct. The trouble is that society often considers it safest to apply heroic measures to simple situations. We use drugs to decrease minor fevers. We turn to major antibiotics every time a person has a head cold. We use antidepressants to cope with normal grief or situational anxiety. Not only do doctors prescribe drugs for acute care, patients also ask for these drugs by name (they've seen them advertised) because they live in a state of constant fear of a disaster that might possibly happen if . . . There's a sense that nature must be controlled and overcome. There's a lack of faith in the wisdom of the body.

Somehow I don't think you are surprised by this logic. You are probably reading this book partly because you are aware that new, equally disturbing health problems have replaced the ones we removed. Epidemics of acute infectious diseases, like measles and polio, have been replaced by epidemics of chronic illnesses, such as asthma, cancer, irritable bowel syndrome, and even obesity. We are facing antibiotic-resistant infections for which doctors still recommend the use of powerful antibiotics.

A Better Approach

As a society, we managed to ignore the big picture for more than a century. Now we are learning that we were prodding a sophisticated, gentle device called a human being with coarse, unsophisticated tools. Although these tools brought us some temporary relief, they in fact ended up causing us more complex, systemic health problems.

Think back to the Confucius quote at the beginning of the chapter. Haven't we been swatting at flies with a hatchet? Actually, I'd rather use the analogy of a sledgehammer. We typically beat at our symptoms with a sledgehammer of powerful medications. As symptoms get suppressed, more complicated, deeper-seated problems come out.

Drugs affect entire human beings. While their intended effects suppress the symptoms of disease or kill the intruders, their many other unintended consequences—side effects—can hurt us. We often indirectly cause our bodies damage by jumping into the middle of the fight between the powerful defense forces given to us by Mother Nature (the immune system is only one of them) and an intruder.

What steps, if any, can we take today to undo the potential harm, as well as the clear and present harm, of overmedicating ourselves? First, we have to stop panicking. It is important to consider our methods of health care reasonably. We must understand when we truly need to intervene with drugs, surgery, and so on. Second, the rest of the time we can successfully call upon the miracle of homeopathy, a method of health care that gives us the freedom to eliminate illness using our own nature-given devices.

The Four Levels of Health

How can you and your family begin to achieve optimal health? Developing a reasonable and trustworthy health care strategy that blends conventional medicine and homeopathy becomes much easier if you understand the four possible levels of health.[1]

Level 1 Health

In *The Jungle Book*, Rudyard Kipling tells the story of a boy living in harmony with nature:

> *Now you must be content to . . . guess at all the wonderful life that Mowgli led among the wolves. . . . He grew up with the cubs . . . and Father Wolf taught him his business, and the meaning of things in the jungle. . . . When he was not learning he sat out in the sun and slept, and ate, and went to sleep again; when he felt dirty or hot he swam in the forest pools; and when he wanted honey . . . he climbed up for it. . . . And he grew and grew strong as a boy must grow, who does not know that he is learning any lessons.[2]*

A city dweller myself, I am far from suggesting that everyone has to live with the wolves in order to be healthy. The important point in my interpretation of the story is that Mowgli grew up strong because he was in constant contact with nature. His body learned quickly what was a friend or an enemy. Although Kipling wasn't specifically writing about it, Mowgli's body would have had no confusion, no allergic reactions. The only help available to the child was good advice from Father Wolf and a few other animals. His body would have been perfectly able to deal with the adversities of daily life. If Mowgli had a cut, he would have had to deal with it. Maybe Baloo, the brown bear, would offer him some herbs to speed the healing. If he had a cold, he would have had to deal with it. Maybe Bagheera, the black panther, would bring him some honey to speed his recovery.

We rarely see this level of health in city dwellers. But I can easily imagine a shepherd from the Alps or a cowboy possessing a strong immune system and having no health problems, even in old age. These people represent the first level of health. Strong and resilient, they are fully capable of dealing with seasonal infections and minor traumas without needing constant support from antibiotics and painkillers. They haven't been exposed to the devastating attacks of noise, chemical pollution, and emotional strain so readily provided by our civilization. We all strive to be at this level of health, but few children of the industrial world are.

All the supplements and vitamins we take and all the dieting and exercise to which we subject ourselves have one ultimate goal: to make us healthy and achieve the magical level of wellness. People with level 1 health recover completely from acute problems. They have chronic diseases neither of the body nor of the mind. If they develop any difficulties during recovery, a single dose of a homeopathic remedy brings them right back to where they were before.

When people grow up surrounded by nature and then become city dwellers, their ability to resist illness remains strong for many years even after they have encountered the adversities and stresses of the industrialized world. Why? Because their major defense systems formed under ideal conditions. Their bodies learned how to resist disease by themselves, without the interference of external agents or pollutants and also without the unnecessary suppression of symptoms by powerful drugs.

Prior to the introduction of chemical and psychological pollutants in daily life, the majority of the population that survived different disease epidemics most likely was at the first level of health. For a few generations after industrialization, humans were able to resist the negative impact of man-made pollutants, but a consistent and powerful widespread assault ultimately brought about a collective decrease in our resistance. We are rapidly moving down the ladder of health.

Let's see what's awaiting us, the dwellers of the so-called civilized world of the twenty-first century, at the second level of health.

Level 2 Health

The classic short story "Hygeia at the Solito" by O. Henry is one of my favorites, as it so clearly illustrates how people with level 2 health are capable of shifting to level 1. In the tale, Cricket McGuire, described as an "ex-feather-weight prizefighter, tout, jockey, follower of the 'ponies,' all-round sport, and manipulator of the gumballs and walnut shells," has been diagnosed with tuberculosis and given an estimated six months to live. Then, altruistic cattleman Curtis Raidler—the picture of robust health and vitality, both physically and emotionally—rescues him by speeding him off to his ranch. "Thus was instituted the reign of terror at the Solito Ranch."[3]

McGuire, a truly heinous individual, sits in his room with the windows closed, smoking cigarettes and trying to figure out a way to scam everyone around him. He is ornery and egotistical and complains nonstop. This goes on for two months, during which time he doesn't improve. Yes, he's got lung disease, but he's also strong and wiry. If it weren't for his chronic cough, you might believe he was a fairly healthy, if unpleasant, individual.

Raidler offers the man some level 1 health care advice. "Try more air, son. . . . The ground, and the air next to it—them's the things to cure you. . . . Close to the ground—that's where the medicine in the air stays. Try a little hossback riding now." When this counsel is rejected, Raidler begins to be suspicious. One evening, he asks a dinner guest—a physician—to examine McGuire.

Another thing I like about this story is that a major plot twist comes from a doctor making a mistake. "In ten minutes the doctor came briskly out. 'Your man,' he said promptly, 'is as sound as a new dollar. . . . I advise you to set him digging post-holes or breaking mustangs.'" Of course, he has examined the wrong man.

Raidler takes his advice. "'Take this man,' said Raidler to Ross Hargis, 'and put him to work. Make him work hard, sleep hard, and eat hard.'" From obstinacy McGuire doesn't correct their illusion and just goes along. The rancher goes off to take care of family business in another state and doesn't return for two months, at which point he comes home, discovers the doctor's error, and is persuaded that McGuire must be dead. He races out to the encampment, where he learns that McGuire is thriving. The doctor's mistake was his salvation. Fresh air, exercise, and simple food were what he needed.

Of course, I would not go so far as to suggest treating tuberculosis with exercise in the prairies. But as you can see from the story, people who have level 2 health are normally healthy people—the primary readership of this book! Typically, they are overworked, stressed, and victims of pollution. Although the body fights against viruses, it wins in the long term, not immediately.

There's an old joke that applies to this group. A common cold goes away in fourteen days with treatment and in two weeks without treatment. But these odds can be improved. Level 2 people can shift to level 1 with the use of homeopathy, because it stimulates self-healing and restoration of powerful defenses.

Level 3 Health

Level 3 health describes chronically ill people who have one or more serious illnesses, such as ongoing asthma and chronic ulcers. Where level 1 people might get colds once or twice a year and level 2 people might get colds several times a year, level 3 people rarely get colds, because their defenses are overstimulated and always operating on high alert. It's like having a firewall up on your computer—anything that enters the system just gets burned up.

Whereas at level 2 the situation is not life threatening, at level 3 it has the potential to be. The goal of homeopathic treatment, which must be provided by trained professionals once you're dealing with this category of ill health, is to help people advance to level 2. If they develop an acute problem, it creates a window of opportunity to improve their overall level of health, as it reveals new symptoms.

At the beginning of the chapter, I explained that there is only one perfect homeopathic remedy for each person at a given time. The process of homeopathy is always to identify the special remedy that matches an individual's unique picture of symptoms. As you read Chapters 4 through 10, you'll find descriptions of the leading indicators for the different homeopathic remedies.

Level 4 Health

Terminally ill people fall into this category. As their defenses are completely exhausted, the body succumbs to the illness. The best we can do for them is offer palliation. This group of people requires sophisticated, complicated treatment, which is far beyond the scope of this book. They should be under the care of a professional.

The Goal of Homeopathy

The primary focus of this book is the treatment of acute ailments, which may be handled differently by people at the different levels of health. How so? And to what purpose?

Healthy people can sustain significant amounts of emotional and environmental stress, including viruses and bacteria. After a short and efficient struggle, which may produce a high fever and other temporarily debilitating symptoms, a healthy person (level 1) eliminates the illness completely and returns to perfect health. He or she rarely needs help to feel better. Such a person may decide to take it easy for a couple of days or can take one dose of a homeopathic remedy and will rapidly recover. This applies to healthy adults, children, and infants.

Most of us, however, live on the second level of health. We are striving to move up by improving our resilience. Effective homeopathic self-care can help us to achieve this goal both by treating our illnesses and by helping us to avoid the unwanted complications of suppressive conventional drug treatment.

People with serious chronic illnesses (level 3) and those who have so far been unable to find a homeopathic solution for acute problems will benefit from professional homeopathic help and can gradually move to the second and even the first level of health.

Now that you have a clearer understanding of the four levels of health, you are ready to learn the basic rules of homeopathy. Which remedy needs to be taken and which type of medical intervention needs to be sought both depend on a person's particular situation at the moment. The levels of health are just a simple tool to help you begin to assess your needs and set realistic expectations.

Basic Rules of Homeopathy

The privilege of a lifetime is being who you are.

—JOSEPH CAMPBELL

WHAT IMAGE COMES TO mind when you think about homeopathy? Maybe you are looking for a magic potion that will transform you—*poof!* Perhaps you are worrying that I'm going to ask you to give up coffee and alcohol, eat only granola and sprouts, and wear Birkenstock sandals year-round. Maybe you've heard that homeopaths are alchemists or belong to a religious cult that's survived in secret since the Middle Ages. I can assure you that none of these notions are accurate, except that homeopathy—upon occasion—cures acute ailments as astonishingly quickly and effectively as a magic elixir would. Often the positive effects of taking a remedy are felt within only a few minutes.

Homeopathic treatment is sophisticated and highly individualized. In this chapter, you'll learn basic principles that will help you choose the precise remedy for a particular problem in a particular individual. Ignoring these basic, easy-to-understand principles will lead you to failure. To succeed in selecting the right remedy, however, all you need to do is spend a few minutes reading and then apply your common sense.

This surprisingly elegant form of medicine is grounded in seven main principles that were discovered and innovated as a result of reproducible clinical experiments and through many years of observation. Let's learn about them now in the order that their significance was established.

Fighting Fire with Fire: The Principle of Similars

The maxim "Fight fire with fire" happens to be absolutely accurate when applied to the process of natural healing. Dr. Hahnemann discovered homeopathy while experimenting with an herbal medicine known as Peruvian bark (also called *China* or *Cinchona*) that was popular in his day for treating malaria. When he took repeated doses of this substance, he noticed that symptoms identical to the symptoms of malaria appeared in his body. And when he stopped taking the medicine, the symptoms gradually went away. After repeating his experiment on a later date and getting the same result, Hahnemann decided to continue experimenting in this fashion with other substances.

In 1796, after six years of thorough experimentation and a literature search, Hahnemann published an article in German in which he proclaimed the discovery of a law of nature: "like cures the like." In essence, he suggested that if there were a substance that in healthy, sensitive individuals caused symptoms similar to what a particular patient had, that substance would cure this patient.

That same year, British physician Edward Jenner published his seminal work on vaccination. (*Vacca* means "cow" in Latin.) Jenner noticed that milkmaids did not have smallpox, but they all had experienced cowpox, a benign condition for humans. He correctly hypothesized that cowpox had been protecting milkmaids from smallpox and suggested that the power of similarity could be harnessed. Thus vaccination was born.

Now it's important to point out that homeopathy is *not* a means of vaccination against various illnesses. However, the idea of similars is the same in both cases. Other important factors on which vaccinations are based differ dramatically from homeopathy.

What you must understand in order to grasp how to select the right homeopathic remedy is that the similarity you're seeking has to be between all the major symptoms and individual characteristics of a sick person and all the symptoms known to be caused by the raw substance from which the remedy is derived in healthy volunteers. It is not a similarity between the diagnoses of different sick people. How those healthy volunteers, called provers, were studied is described in the discussion of the next principle.

Let's compare. Vaccinations are the same for all individuals, regardless of their unique characteristics. But two different people with the same diagnosis—for example, of a diagnosis of seasonal allergies—are likely to receive two different homeopathic remedies.

Here's something that could happen in real life. Two people are in the final stages of completing a book together about homeopathy. One becomes extremely edgy, asks everyone to speak quietly, and yells at people when they don't do things his way. He wakes up every night at 3 A.M., thinking about the work, and cannot get back to sleep. He also starts feeling cold constantly and craves coffee and spicy food. Uncharacteristically, he wants to drink alcohol. He also becomes constipated and has a feeling of incompleteness after a bowel movement. This would be a typical case for the remedy *Nux vomica*, which will be described in Chapter 10.

The other author on the project works just as hard as the first author and as a result feels totally drained. He cannot think about anything. All he needs is to stop writing and rest. This would be a case for the remedy *Picricum acidum*, which will be described in Chapter 8. I am sure you, the reader, understand that I am not talking about anyone we know. This is just an example of how the need for remedies differs according to the individual person, despite their mutual circumstances or problem.

The two preceding presentations are obviously different, and, if you know the characteristics that require treatment from a specific remedy, the results are amazing.

Conventional medicine strives to achieve the same level of precision in treating individual patients. In medical parlance, the approach is called differential therapeutics. But only homeopathic practitioners have been able to master this technique so far.

The Principle of Proving

This word for an experiment conducted to catalog the homeopathic qualities of a raw substance comes from the German word *prüfüng*, which means "test." Hahnemann conducted the first proving when he took Peruvian bark. Luckily for us, he happened to be sensitive to this raw substance, because he developed symptoms from taking it and ultimately discovered homeopathy. Not all provers have similar sensitivities.

The process of proving closely resembles the technique that forensic sketch artists and police profilers use to create a composite picture of a criminal. Witnesses choose a shape for the face, a type of hair, eyes, and all other features from a large library offered by a computer. Put together, these separate features borrowed from various people create a virtual portrait of the perpetrator of a crime.

A virtual picture of the ideal prover, a person who would be sensitive to every aspect of the remedy being tested, is also created as a composite from the symptoms presented by various individual provers. By testing many sensitive people, the process identifies the totality of symptoms that this particular raw substance could possibly induce. Frequently, there is an ideal prover who develops most, or even all, of the possible symptoms that the substance may induce in a human being. Of course, there are also people who have no sensitivity to a given substance whatsoever.

This idea of sensitivity and insensitivity shouldn't come as a surprise to you. After all, some people cannot tolerate coffee, some are sensitive to cat dander, while others can eat and drink anything they like and gladly keep five cats in the house.

After a remedy has been proven, the data that's been gathered is entered in a systematic, uniform way into a book called the *Materia Medica*. Nowadays such books are computerized to make them more easily searchable. A homeopath also needs to have personal experience with the remedies. Many symptoms listed in *Materia Medica* have been derived from clinical experience. For example, famous nineteenth-century homeopath Adolph Lippe noticed that the homeopathic remedy *Phosphorus* cured the kind of nausea that develops after cold water that a patient drank a few minutes earlier gets warm in the stomach. This symptom is recorded in every homeopathic book, including this one. Yet it did not come up in provings.

As you can perhaps imagine, each remedy that a homeopath has personally studied and used successfully becomes alive in his or her imagination. We all carry virtual images of people possessing unique sets of characteristics that correspond to a particular remedy. That is why homeopaths frequently make statements like *"Nux vomica* is better from warm applications" or *"Pulsatilla nigricans* needs consolation." It's as though the remedy is a person.

Obviously, homeopaths don't think that a given remedy is alive, but it does have thousands of unique characteristics that add up to an emerging quality or imaginative vision of a virtual person—sometimes a person we have met. But don't worry when you're selecting remedies for home aid. This level of sophistication, although highly desirable, is not a requirement for the successful application of a few basic remedies for common acute conditions. All you need to be able to do is look for clear symptoms and compare them to the clearly defined symptoms of remedies described in this book.

As you read through this book, you'll notice that I often talk about the *"Gelsemium* state," or the *"Aconitum* state." Homeopaths define our patients as being in the state of a particular remedy if the totality of their symptoms matches the totality of the symptoms that were elicited during a proving. The proving helps us apply the principle of similars.

The Principle of Individualized Treatment

This concept should be pretty obvious from everything you've just read. Because the process of selecting the remedy consists of paying attention to details, the final decision is made based on the combination of characteristics unique to a given person. What characteristics are important? In acute conditions, the most important symptoms are those that appeared as a result of the illness.

Here's an example. A person falls to the ground after being hit by a car. As you approach him, you see that he is bleeding. But he says, "I'm OK. I don't need any help. Let me just rest for a few minutes, and then I'll be on my way to work." This is a unique and remarkable symptom. He thinks he is OK despite obvious and fairly severe problems. It is the combination of these two things—severe trauma and this nonchalant approach to a dangerous situation—that clearly point to the homeopathic remedy *Arnica* (see Chapter 5).

In another case I witnessed, two cars collided, and a bleeding man jumped out of one car and started running around and screaming murder. He was scared! No one could calm him down. This was a typical case requiring *Aconitum* (see Chapter 4).

You see, there was trauma in both cases, but each accident victim was clearly experiencing a different mental and emotional state. Furthermore, as you may have noticed, in both cases I only described emotional reactions and made a selection of the remedy without even going into detailed physical complaints. Homeopaths know that if there is a clear emotional component to the presentation, it has to be taken very seriously, and it frequently dictates the prescription of the remedy. The reason is that the emotional state is the result of the totality of processes going on in the rest of the body. This is the first and most important indicator in choosing a remedy.

The next important indicator for choosing the remedy is called generalities. These are the symptoms that reflect how a person reacts to the stress of the problem in the rest of his or her body. For example, a person may feel better in a cold environment or in a warm environment. She may feel better in the morning and worse in the afternoon. Some people become thirsty, and others don't want to drink even during fever. (This is peculiar, isn't it?) For example, people who need *Nux vomica*, the remedy described in Chapter 10, are highly sensitive to cold and also frequently wake up unrefreshed. On the other hand, people who need *Sulphur* are always hot and thirsty for cold water.

The next most important factor to consider is modalities. Those are precise things that make a symptom better or worse. For example, some people's coughs are exacerbated by lying down, and in others their coughs are made worse by even the slightest motion. Some individuals cough almost exclusively after walking out into the cold air. Some cough from walking into a warm room. All these important points will be clearly described in this book for each remedy. They make finding the remedy rather easy.

If you can see them, that is.

The Principle of Single Remedy

I simply love the old adage "If there is more than one answer to a question, there is no answer." Classical homeopaths would agree. The particular state of a particular patient corresponds to one particular remedy. You should always do your best to find it.

Of course, everyone is human and makes mistakes. And that is OK. If the remedy you choose does not work, you can always try another one that you think is the next best choice. One practice would be wrong, however: simply throwing one remedy after the other at someone without carefully analyzing that person's unique characteristics!

An opposite technique is to give all the remedies with similar characteristics to someone hoping that one of them might work. This approach is also inherently wrong. Just think about it. A person is suffering from a cold that is characterized by the person feeling sedated and disoriented. Her pupils are large, her head is hot, and her hands are cold. She seems confused. To me (and to you, soon, after you read Chapter 6), hers is a clear case for *Belladonna*. If one of the geniuses that propagate a combined use of many remedies decides to give the patient *Belladonna* and *Aconitum* together, it would make no sense. The two remedies will ultimately work against each other because their characteristics are so different and the ill person is so vulnerable. She could even become worse from exposure to the confusing combined characteristics of the two remedies.

And what if someone suggests giving more remedies? The situation becomes even more confusing. Both trying remedies in rapid succession and giving multiple remedies at once are forms of polypharmacy. Single dosing is more effective.

In principle, conventional medicine is also against polypharmacy. Unfortunately, the reality of life is different. It is practiced not only by conventional doctors but also by some homeopathic practitioners.

Less Is More: The Principle of Minimal Dose (How to Take Remedies)

Take as small an effective dose as possible. This concept is simple and very logical. Homeopathic remedies stimulate an innate capacity that we all have: the capacity to cure. The moment the process is on its way, there is no reason to push further. If you do, the result will swing the opposite way: you might create a proving (that is, add more symptoms to your condition that are characteristic to the remedy).

Traditionally, homeopathic remedies are sold in the form of either pellets or a liquid extract, an alcohol-based tincture. The pellets are more popular and generally easier to store and dispense. Their base material is a mixture of sucrose and lactose, which is combined with a small drop of an 88 percent alcohol solution of the remedy. The pellets are thoroughly shaken to distribute the solution evenly. While tinctures taste slightly bitter, pellets are sweet. They are safe for chemically sensitive individuals and diabetics.

To take a remedy, place the pellets under your tongue. If you are using a remedy in liquid form, either put the drops directly in your mouth or dilute it in a small amount of water and then drink it. The rule of thumb is to take, or give, one dose and then wait for fifteen minutes. If there is significant improvement, wait. Repeat the dose only if you, or the person taking the remedy, begin to feel worse again.

If the healing effect is partial or the symptoms are severe (for example, as in the case of an accident or a trauma), you can repeat the remedy a few times. The length of the intervals between such repeated doses varies. It should be shorter for worse conditions. In the case of a massive motor vehicle accident, repeat your dose every five to ten minutes. In the case of a bad flu or cold, repeat your dose at fifteen- to thirty-minute intervals as usual.

Do not take a repeat dose if there is no effect at all.

Stop giving doses when the person feels 50 to 60 percent better.

Along with pellets and tinctures, homeopathic remedies are produced in the forms of ointments, lotions, and gels, which can be applied externally, cell salts (see page 26), and as suppositories. These have less therapeutic effect than the internally consumed remedies.

Babies younger than one year of age have undeveloped swallowing mechanisms, so an alternate method of giving remedies must be used. The technique I recommend is known as the plussing method. To do it, place three pellets of a concentration 30C remedy in a small bottle of springwater from which you have spilled out about a third of the contents. Replace the lid. Let the remedy sit in the water for about five minutes. Then vigorously shake the bottle a few times, like you would a container of orange juice. Giving the baby a teaspoon of this water constitutes one dose. Store the bottle at room temperature. It will remain good for two days. Shake before use. The plussing method is occasionally useful for adults as well, in cases when you would prefer to administer a remedy in a liquid form.

Another, more "material," way to administer homeopathy to babies than the plussing method is to crush three pellets of a concentration 30C remedy between two spoons, add a drop of water, and spoon feed the mixture to the child.

The Taming of the Shrew: The Principle of Homeopathic Potencies

There is one extremely controversial issue involved in the practice of homeopathic medicine: ultramolecular dilutions. These remedies show no trace of molecules of the raw substances from which they are derived. Critics habitually accuse homeopaths of tricking their patients into taking a placebo.

Common definitions of placebo are as follows:

* A substance containing no medication and prescribed or given to reinforce a patient's expectation to get well
* Something of no intrinsic remedial value that is used to appease or reassure another[1]

Homeopaths and millions of patients cured by homeopathy maintain that remedies are active. A simple point of consideration in support of homeopathy is that infants and animals respond well to it. To this the critics reply that even animals may experience a placebo effect if they like their caregiver.

Another simple argument in favor of homeopathy is that a placebo usually produces different effects in different people, while homeopathic remedies consistently induce the same results in provings. Multiple provings and reprovings of many remedies have been done. The skeptics doubt that it's true.

To prove the point further, homeopaths have presented impressive statistics of the successful treatment of patients during various epidemics, including the great success during the flu pandemic of 1918, which struck a few continents. Quite a few well-designed clinical studies confirm that remedies cause an effect statistically different from placebo.[2]

Since Hahnemann, homeopathic practitioners around the world have routinely prescribed remedies in concentrations that do not contain detectable doses of substances—at least not detectable by current technologies. One obvious advantage of this practice is that homeopaths can employ all the positive benefits of otherwise poisonous substances without being concerned about causing harm to their patients. In a sense, homeopathic methods of preparation "tame the shrew."

To be fair, the majority of substances used to engender homeopathic remedies are not poisonous in any way. Some are, in fact, chemically inert in their crude forms. For example, *Natrum muriaticum*—a powerful homeopathic remedy that's frequently used to treat migraine headaches, depression, and other chronic problems—is made out of table salt. So homeopathy has it both ways. Due to the field's particular method of processing substances, we can utilize positive healing qualities of both poisons and inert substances.

The exact process that led Hahnemann to develop high-dilution remedies is unknown. One generally accepted theory is that he saw that less-diluted preparations in some cases caused an initial worsening of the condition. In homeopathic parlance, this phenomenon is called an aggravation. Subsequent attempts to dilute the remedies in combination with vigorous shaking, however, brought out remedies that, on one hand, were harmless and, on the other hand, caused deep and long-lasting cures. His preferred method became to alternate dilution and shaking throughout a many-step process.

In the preparation of homeopathic remedies, the process of vigorous shaking between each step of dilution is important. It is called potentization. Remarkably, a famous study by Professor Jacques Benveniste, which will be described on page 27, clearly demonstrated that a homeopathic serial dilution with potentization at each step produces a biologically active substance. The same substance diluted without shaking is biologically inactive.

How exactly are homeopathic remedies made? Remedies come in two main concentrations: decimal (diluted 1:10 at each step) and centesimal (diluted 1:100 at each step). Decimal dilutions are either labeled with the Latin number *X* (meaning "10") or, in some countries, a *D* (from *decimal*). Centesimal dilutions are labeled with the Latin number *C* (meaning "100").

Between each step of dilution, the container holding the remedy that's being prepared is vigorously shaken ten to twenty times. Originally, Hahnemann simply held a tube in his fist and hit it vigorously against a thick leather-bound book (actually, it was a Bible). Nowadays a machine called a potentizer imitates the same motion. The process of hitting the container is called succussion. In homeopathic parlance, one would say that each dilution involves ten to twenty succussions.

Here's a real example of how dilution and succussion are done:

1. To prepare *Belladonna* 1C, a pharmacist takes one part of an original tincture of the plant and ninety-nine parts of alcohol and mixes them in a tube. The mixture is then succussed ten times. The resulting concentration is 10^{-2}.
2. To create 2C, a pharmacist takes one part of 1C and dilutes it in ninety-nine parts of alcohol by applying ten succussions. The resulting concentration is 10^{-4}. The total number of succussions is twenty.

The process of the preparation of decimal dilutions is similar, except each step is a 1:10 dilution. The number of succussions at each step remains the same.

Homeopaths call dilutions potencies, because remedies become stronger and longer- and deeper-acting as a result of combining dilution with succussion.

The strength-dilution paradox has been disturbing to conventional physicians, who, as I explained, often accuse homeopaths of offering their patients placebos. The problem became even more serious in 1909, when chemists realized that at 12C, a homeopathic concentration that equals dilution 10^{-24} (and 120 succussions), the original substance disappears.[3]

In practice, homeopaths routinely use the potencies shown in Table 2.1.

Cell salts are made from insoluble minerals using a process known as trituration that was devised by Hahnemann to convert insoluble materials into a soluble form that could be introduced into the core homeopathic process. A German doctor, Wilhelm Schuessler, popularized twelve basic mineral preparations in 3X, 6X, 12X, and 30X concentrations. These are less frequently used by classical homeopaths than pellets and tinctures.

In 1988 a three-page scientific paper published in *Nature* magazine provoked a significant controversy and a scientific scandal.[4] The research team whose work it described came from France, Israel, Italy, and Canada and was led by Professor Jacques Benveniste, who at the time worked at the highly regarded French National Institute for Scientific Research in Medicine (INSERM), which is the French equivalent of the U.S. National Institutes of Health. The paper reported that an extremely high dilution of immunoglobulin prepared homeopathically still stimulated the function of basophils, cells that are an important part of a person's immune system.

The only plausible explanation to this phenomenon offered by the research team was that homeopathic preparation of various substances leads to changes in the structure of water, which then affect the body. This phenomenon was named the memory of water. Unfor-

Table 2.1 Homeopathic Dilutions

CENTECIMAL			DECIMAL	
Potency	Dilution	Total number of succusions	Potency	Dilution
6C	10^{-12}	60	6X	10^{-6}
12C	10^{-24}	120	12X	10^{-12}
30C	10^{-60}	300	30X	10^{-30}
200C	10^{-400}	2,000		
1M	$10^{-2,000}$	20,000		
10M	$10^{-20,000}$	100,000		
50M	$10^{-100,000}$	500,000		

tunately, the conclusion was too revolutionary. The results of the study were highly criticized. Benveniste's lab was investigated by a team that included the editor of *Nature* and a magician (I am not kidding) who was also a well-known opponent of homeopathy. Despite the fact that researchers in four separate countries independently had conducted the study and achieved the same results, the research protocols were deemed "irreproducible." The study was proclaimed fraudulent. Benveniste lost his position at INSERM.

A combination of a bad precedent with an extremely challenging hypothesis made this issue a scientific taboo. As recently as 2005, I attempted to discuss these studies with a young gifted physicist who works in a prestigious biological research institution. He told me point-blank that the subject was "closed for discussion" between us due to the "inconceivable" premise that a pill containing no material substance can be active.

Ironically, in 2004, the year Benveniste passed away, the members of his original team published the results of another sophisticated study that once again demonstrated that homeopathically prepared ultramolecular dilutions are biologically active.[5]

Hering's Principle of Cure

Dr. Constantine Hering, the man considered to be the father of American homeopathy, is credited with formally stating a phenomenon that has been observed by numerous homeopaths, beginning with Hahnemann. Hering's principle of cure explains that the process of healing symptoms happens concurrently in the following four dimensions:

* **From above downward.** Healing starts from the head and ends at the feet.
* **From within outward.** Healing starts from the internal organs and moves to the skin.
* **From a more important organ to a less important one.** A person's heart or liver would heal before the digestive tract or skin.

❊ **In the reverse order of their coming.** Working chronologically backward through time, the healing of more recent problems precedes the healing of problems from years, even decades, earlier.

Hering's principle of cure is especially important to consider when you're engaged in the treatment of long-standing, or chronic, conditions, as these are usually multifaceted. In the application of homeopathy to acute conditions, the improvement is usually prompt. An acute illness is a short-lived condition with symptoms that are different from the usual characteristics of the person.

Safety and Quality Control

Homeopathic remedies have been in continuous use since the early 1800s. Throughout the entire period, there have been no reliable reports of poisonings. As you saw just a few pages ago, the substances they contain are highly diluted. In July 2005, I nonetheless conducted a thorough literature search and discovered no incidences of toxicity caused by homeopathic preparations that were correctly used according to the standards of practice. Even in cases of the incorrect and predictably dangerous use of remedies in potentially toxic concentrations, there were only two reports of complications due to homeopathic preparations. One of these incidents occurred in India when somebody used repeated doses of *Arsenicum album* in homeopathic concentration 1X, which was a foolish decision.[6] This concentration is a material dose, rather than a highly diluted dose of arsenic.

In Europe and America, homeopathy is regulated by the strict standards of each country's own homeopathic pharmacopoeia. The Homeopathic Pharmacopoeia of the United States (HPUS) has been an instrument of the Federal Food, Drug, and Cosmetic Act since 1938. The Food and Drug Administration (FDA) in 1988 restated the legality of using homeopathic remedies, which are regulated as over-the-counter medications.[7]

According to HPUS, arsenic trioxide must not be used in potencies lower than 4C or 8X, a diluted amount equal to ten parts per billion. If you are mathematically inclined, you can easily calculate that this concentration equals ten nanograms (10^{-8} of a gram) per gram of the final product. By way of comparison, public health regulations allow drinking water to contain fifty parts of arsenic per billion. Although 4C and 8X potencies share the same concentrations of the original substance used to produce the remedy, 8X remedies have been shaken (succused) twice as much as 4C remedies (see Table 2.1 on page 27).

Another report comes from Mexico. Unfortunately, the only information available in English is from the abstract. It states that an infant with diaper rash, a mild respiratory infection, and diarrhea was treated with *Mercurius* 6X (dilution 10^{-6}). According to this report, the infant became seriously ill with an exacerbation and spreading of the rash, as well as irritability and protein in the urine. Conventional treatment resolved the issue.[8]

Again, the use of such a highly concentrated preparation made from mercury is unusual. By commonly accepted international standards of conventional homeopathic practice, it should not have been used in a baby in a concentration lower than 6C (dilution 10^{-12}).

So you see, this case doesn't apply to the rules of homeopathy that you will be guided to follow in this book.

Interestingly, there are numerous reports of well-designed animal studies in which homeopathy was shown to prevent and treat both arsenic and mercury toxicity.[9]

While the danger of you or your family members experiencing a direct toxic effect from a raw substance used to prepare a homeopathic remedy is close to zero, you should be aware that the unnecessary repetition of a remedy might cause a proving. In reality, that is exactly how provings are accomplished: healthy volunteers take repeated doses of a homeopathic preparation until they develop symptoms, which are then cataloged for posterity. At that point the administration of the remedy stops.

To be safe in your at-home use of homeopathy, just remember not to repeat the remedy as long as there is an improvement in the condition you are treating. Taking more of a good thing is not better. Your rule of thumb is to take no more than three doses of your remedy at fifteen- to thirty-minute intervals. As long as the patient is getting better—whether that means for an hour, a day, a week, or a year—do not repeat the dose. If you follow these simple instructions, everyone in your household will be protected.

How to Find the Right Remedy

When you turn to this book's chapters about the different homeopathic remedies, you'll come to lists and comparison tables cataloging their leading characteristics. Use these as signposts to guide you in the selection of a remedy for a particular problem. Your goal is to match the picture of the remedy to the person who will receive it.

Please follow these four rules:

1. Base your choice only on clear, apparent symptoms. Do not try to find the symptoms of the remedy that you *wish* would be the correct choice.
2. Do not choose a remedy if its core symptom (for example, restless panic for *Aconitum* or irritability for *Nux vomica*) is not present.
3. Do not try to discern mental symptoms if they are not there. Sometimes the need for a remedy is purely physical.
4. Do not make things complicated. The seven main remedies in this book fit a large proportion of cases. Consider them first. In some cases, I will indicate that another remedy is a more common medication for the particular problem being evaluated. But if the symptoms you have don't fit the picture of one of those two remedies, continue looking through the alternatives offered in the corresponding section.

Some Other Important Things to Remember

Keep the following additional guidelines in mind:

1. Do not pay too much attention to stories you might hear about various substances, such as mint or coffee, counteracting your remedy. First of all, you will be taking the remedy for only a short period of time, to treat an acute condition. Second, most of the substances claimed to be bad for homeopathy actually are not. Warnings about mint are a glaring example of this type of misinformation. The reason behind the advice is simple. Mint creates a cool feeling in your mouth by collapsing capillaries, the smallest blood vessels. But you need the capillaries to be open when you take your remedy so it can be absorbed. Truth is that the moment the remedy dissolves you are in the clear. Mint only temporarily blocks absorption, it does not reverse the effects of homeopathic remedies. So go ahead and eat your mint candies or your mint chocolate ice cream.

There are special homeopathic brands of toothpaste that do not contain mint, although they do contain combinations of remedies. And those remedies wind up right where they could affect the action of the remedy you are presently using—in your mouth. So please feel free to use regular toothpaste, just ensure that you take the remedy at least a few minutes before or an hour after you have brushed your teeth.

Experience has shown that coffee and camphor-containing rubs counteract homeopathy. It's not known why—that's just the way it is. Large amounts of dark chocolate do the same thing that coffee does. If you drink coffee, eat dark chocolate, or use a camphor-containing rub, wait for two to three hours and then take your remedy. If you drink alcohol in large amounts or frequently, or if you habitually use marijuana or other street drugs, homeopathy may not work for you.

2. Do not store homeopathic remedies near electrical or electronic devices. Strong electromagnetic fields make homeopathy inactive. Going through the metal detector at the airport seems to be OK, however.

3. Do not get carried away by the idea of homeopathic vaccinations, as there are very few situations in which homeopathy has been known to act prophylactically. If you do get carried away, you'll wind up frequently using multiple powerful homeopathic remedies (polypharmacy), and this is not a good idea at all.

4. Another pretty common misconception is that the homeopathic remedies *Thuja* and *Silicea* can be used to protect children and adults from side effects of vaccines. This would work only for people who needed one of these remedies to treat their chronic problems. This can be decided only by a trained homeopath. Certainly, no remedy should be used without thinking.

5. Please do not feel that you absolutely have to cure every single acute problem you or your family and friends have. You will make mistakes. I still do. And it is OK to make mistakes as long as you don't start giving a lot of remedies one right after another. Simply do your best, and if you failed once, you'll do better the next time. In the meanwhile, go back to conventional drugs and doctors. Do not sacrifice yourself for homeopathy. There are enough professional homeopaths that do that.

You may now begin to use homeopathy to treat simple, acute conditions. In the next chapter, we'll talk about treatment of chronic or complicated acute problems in partnership with trained homeopaths. It is a good idea to get a homeopath on board to counsel you as you are learning what to do, but it's not an imperative. The remedies and guidance in *Easy Homeopathy* provide a tremendous amount of information and support.

Good luck!

3

Your Visit to the Homeopath

"I'm one of the Sole Sanhedrims and Ostensible Hooplas of the Inner Pulpit," says I. "The lame talk and the blind rubber whenever I make a pass at 'em. I am a medium, a coloratura hypnotist and a spirituous control. It was only through me at the recent séances at Ann Arbor that the late president of the Vinegar Bitters Company could revisit the earth to communicate with his sister Jane."

—O. HENRY, *JEFF PETERS AS A PERSONAL MAGNET*

O. HENRY'S DESCRIPTION perfectly fits the profile of a professional homeopath held in the minds of the majority of people who don't know much or anything about the field. Of course, that's not your understanding now, provided you've read the first two chapters. Even so, you may be surprised at what happens during a typical homeopathic evaluation, as well as by the types of questions a homeopath asks and, more important, doesn't ask. Many people have heard that homeopathy solves chronic health issues, and possibly they even know someone who was cured by a homeopath. Nonetheless, the inner workings of the homeopathic kitchen, so to speak, remain a mystery to them. This chapter, therefore, will address the realities of professional homeopathic practice.

In my experience, a large proportion of those who go to see a homeopath for the first time in their lives don't really know what to expect from treatment: how long it lasts, how homeopaths arrive at a particular remedy, what type of information the homeopathic practitioner considers, or how homeopathy interacts with other methods of treatment (both conventional and nonconventional). Very importantly, they also don't know how to find a good homeopathic practitioner.

Let's talk about these and other issues.

What Homeopathy Can and Can't Do for You and Your Family

First things first. What can and can't homeopathy do? In a small box, the answer is simple and clear. Homeopathy helps cure illnesses that result from potentially reversible malfunctions of the mind or the body. By this definition, a serious condition like depression or chronic asthma or even a peptic ulcer may be cured, because in such cases, there is no permanent damage to the structural components of the body. Of course, no form of treatment known to us today can help to grow a new set of teeth or a new limb.

It is easy to appreciate the difference between these two types of situations (reversible and nonreversible), but what about conditions like cancer or serious, chronic illnesses for which a person goes to a homeopath while taking one or more conventional medications. Will homeopathy work?

The main issue in whether homeopathic treatment is going to be successful is not how advanced or severe an illness is, or what a person is taking for it, but how clearly a practitioner is able to identify the correct matching remedy to prescribe for it.

Providers of all kinds of alternative medicine are acutely aware of the fact that people often come to them with the expectations of an outcome close to a miracle, and the providers feel that they should deliver nothing short of a miracle every time they treat a patient. Homeopaths feel this way because we do get to see miracles, for real—but not each and every time. We see the miracle of cure only when the selection of a remedy is 100 percent accurate: when the entire unique picture of symptoms characteristic to the remedy fits the entire picture of the illness in a particular individual, the patient. Quite often, achieving such precision in prescribing is not a one-shot deal. It requires an effort, not only on the part of the homeopath but also on the part of the patient. Several visits may be required and several months may pass as the correct remedy is approached.

Another important factor in success is how many resources the patient possesses that support recovery. I have met cancer patients who were full of energy and hopes of recovery, and I have met young, strong-looking men who were falling apart and demanding immediate relief from a sore throat. Resources are mental, emotional, and physical, and it can be surprising to discover who has got the most.

Although it would be inaccurate to produce a blanket statement covering all possible cases of illness, the rule of thumb is that there is going to be success in most cases where the physiological root is reversible. When there is no or little functional capacity left, such as in cases of hypothyroidism or insulin-dependent diabetes, we are really only talking about the possibility of decreasing the amount of conventional medications someone needs or palliation of their symptoms.

The Importance of Addressing Your Apparent Diseases

Since the days of Hahnemann, homeopaths have clearly distinguished what is called the apparent disease from other types of symptoms. This expression refers to a situation when the cause of an illness is clear and its removal will lead to a complete cure.

If I were working in an emergency room, and someone walked in with a knife sticking out of his back and told me, "Doc, I need you to cure me, but under no circumstances are you allowed to remove the knife," I wouldn't be able to help.

Yes, modern painkillers could remove the man's pain, but he would ultimately bleed to death or develop an infection that would kill him. To save him, it would be imperative for me to remove the knife, make sure no damage had been done to his internal organs, and suture the wound. Only after that could I promise him a cure.

I'll never forget the case of a middle-aged woman sent to me by referral from another homeopath. She had no appetite and was rapidly losing weight, became weak, and then developed severe digestive problems in combination with significant swelling in her legs. She waited a long time even to see a homeopath because she did not trust doctors. Based on many of the symptoms she presented, this homeopath, who also happens to be a family physician, strongly suspected the possibility of cancer and suggested the woman undergo a thorough medical workup. The patient refused even a regular physical exam. She stated that she did not trust "all these corrupt physicians."

In this case, the homeopath tried a few well-chosen homeopathic remedies, without any effect. The patient was getting worse. Then the homeopath referred her to me. In a phone conversation, we agreed that, based on all the symptoms she was exhibiting so far, a thorough medical workup was important. At the time, I was fortunately working at Beth Israel, a medical center with good nurses. I spent an hour talking to the woman about the necessity of having a physical exam and doing many other studies. She finally agreed to be examined by a nurse. The woman returned to the first homeopath and eventually had some studies done. These showed that she had an advanced stage of cancer. All the tests she needed had been done too late.

The lesson of this unfortunate and not so exceptional case is simple. Doing nothing in cases when you have obviously alarming symptoms is dangerous. It is silly to deny the advances of modern biomedical science and concentrate only on negative information. You need to know what is going on in your body.

Interestingly, the notion that an infection is an apparent disease and that simply killing a "bug" will lead to a cure for an infection is most probably wrong. First of all, not everyone becomes ill even during the worst epidemics of the most terrible illnesses. Second, even the most powerful antibiotics won't cure sick patients in 100 percent of cases. There is very little that antibiotics can do to kill viruses. An infectious disease is always a combination of an intrusion (being infected by bacteria or a virus) and a reaction from the host (a human being or an animal). Homeopathy helps make the host stronger so that the immune system can eliminate the intruder.

In my opinion, regular dental cleanings and checkups, regular physicals, and pediatric or gynecological exams are a must. Knowing what's going on always puts you ahead of the game. Regardless of the diagnosis, you will always be in charge of making a decision about what treatment to use. But you ought to be able to make an *informed* decision.

What You Can Expect During Treatment

I remember my first patient at the Continuum Center for Health and Healing at Beth Israel Medical Center in New York City very well. This Brazilian woman came to me with many serious chronic health issues, including probable infertility, PMS, and emotional problems. We talked about her troubles for two hours, which, by the way, is a perfectly normal length of time for an initial homeopathic evaluation. At the end of the appointment, I started explaining the course of treatment. She interrupted, saying, "Doctor, I grew up with homeopathy. I know that you'll give me only one dose of a highly diluted remedy and make me wait for a month or two before reassessing me."

I was pleasantly surprised. This type of conversation had certainly not been the case with numerous patients I saw before in my practice in New York City. Most New Yorkers want results now, or, preferably, yesterday. Not that immediate results ever happen in real life with any type of treatment. But this is the attitude. Also, people tend to feel that if something is good for you, it must be taken every day, like a vitamin.

My Brazilian patient came back for her follow-up visit a month later and reported that her mood was better, her premenstrual syndrome was 20 to 30 percent better, and her energy level had improved. Then she said, "From what I remember about homeopathy, I'm doing pretty well. There is slight but definite progress."

I was totally blown away by her statement. She truly understood that the healing process, triggered by the homeopathic remedy, was going to proceed at the pace dictated by nature, not by our wishes.

This particular woman went on to improve significantly and, in the course of a year, gave birth to her first baby. Her husband, who became a believer in homeopathy after he saw his wife's improvement, came to see me for himself and was cured of chronic migraine headaches. I lost track of their family a few years ago.

A reality of homeopathic practice is that people get better and then disappear, which is appropriate if they're cured. Unfortunately, many patients who don't get better right away disappear, too. This is a big mistake!

May Homeopathy Be Combined with Other Treatments?

As discussed, finding the exact remedy that fits a particular individual can be difficult. Frequently, the situation is compounded by the fact that in addition to homeopathy, the patient is taking conventional medications and employing many other healing modalities, including vitamin supplements, Chinese herbs, acupuncture, ayurveda, cranial therapy, and so forth. The list of possibilities goes on and on. Homeopaths—or any other health care providers, for that matter—have to rely on their experience to navigate through the chaos of multiple methods of treatment.

A good description of what it's like when various treatments are combined is what happens when two people attempt to row a boat toward different destinations. One wants to go east, the other west. After hours of effort, the rowboat doesn't move an inch or keeps spinning around in circles. Why? The oarsmen are rowing against each other. Similarly, when a person takes several medications, the body's functions work in opposition. It is better to give homeopathy a fair chance to produce a cure without throwing other complementary and alternative interventions into the mix.

The big question is whether homeopathy can do anything for people taking conventional medications. The short answer to this question is yes, it can. Today the majority of the population regularly takes medication of some kind (including stimulants, antidepressants, and heart medications), a figure that is overwhelmingly large especially if you also factor in contraceptives, megadoses of vitamins, and other food supplements.

Of course, homeopaths would love to see patients who take no medications and present clear, easy-to-elicit symptoms. But even if that was typical a hundred years ago, it certainly isn't the situation now, and there are no signs that this state of affairs is going to change soon. Fortunately, modern homeopaths have learned how to handle this issue in most instances of combining conventional medications with homeopathy. However, nature refuses to compromise when it comes to the simultaneous use of hormonal preparations, antibiotics, immunosuppressive drugs, and homeopathy.

If you are on antibiotics, hormones, or immune suppressants and want to explore the possibility of getting homeopathic treatment, please complete the course of your medication first. Then, if your problem still exists and your doctor informs you that you must take a break from those drugs, use the window of opportunity to explore the homeopathic approach.

What Information Is Important?

What can homeopaths do with all the different kinds of information that various other health care providers have offered you? Our approach to any kind of information should be pragmatic. If it helps to find the remedy, we need it. If it can't help us find the remedy, we should disregard it. Spending time talking about nonessential information actually decreases a homeopath's chance to find an appropriate remedy. After all, at least in my practice, the interview can last only for a limited amount of time (although long by conventional standards). So what types of data are important and what are not important?

In my practice, I frequently hear a long list of information that an acupuncturist or ayurvedic doctor told my new patient. Unfortunately, other forms of medicine have little or no information that can be utilized by a homeopath, as our databases are not parallel. I cannot translate a report about weakness of chi in the liver meridian into finding an apt remedy. Telling me about an excess of any of the three doshas will also do me no good. I respect Chinese medicine and ayurveda. I have seen people get good results from them. But there are no practical bridges between them and homeopathy. Homeopathy developed in Western culture and is based on a different theoretical foundation.

What about conventional medical information? Can a homeopath utilize data derived from modern biomedical examination? Yes, with the qualifier, to a certain extent. Here's why.

Both systems—homeopathy and allopathy, or conventional medicine—officially recognize that illness affects the entire human being, but only homeopathy puts this idea into practice. As we all know, specialization is the middle name of modern medicine. Psychologists and psychiatrists stand apart from the other medical specialists who either totally ignore their patients' emotional states or throw an antidepressant at them. A homeopath is acutely aware of the utmost importance of the emotional state created by illness. While conventional medicine emphasizes having a detailed understanding of local changes in different organs and systems of a person's body, such as the brain and nervous system, homeopathy pays more attention to the systemic reaction of the entire human being to the illness, such as migraine headaches.

A patient who suffers from migraine headaches will have to undergo a series of imaging studies of the brain, detailed neurological evaluations, and numerous blood tests. If all of these tests come back negative, a conventional medical doctor will offer the patient a medication based on the rate of success he or she has had in using it for treatment of uncomplicated migraines in the past.

A homeopath will be similarly interested to learn that this patient's headache is not caused by a tumor, a brain hemorrhage, or any other apparent cause but then will want to collect additional data to determine how different this particular individual with headaches is from everyone else with the same diagnosis. The homeopath will ask questions about which side the headache is on, the timing and the triggers of the headache, and the emotional characteristics of the person. Even food desires and aversions will be examined to establish a unique picture of the illness in this particular individual. Those symptoms will then be matched with a remedy. Homoeopathy has a high degree of precision, as provings have been done on more than 2,500 homeopathic remedies.

Hopefully, I've made it clear that while lab work and the results of an MRI are important for developing a good idea of what damage, if any, has been done on a physical level, they still are just small pieces of the health puzzle. A much larger and the most important section of the puzzle for a homeopath is the information about the reaction of the whole human being to the illness or damage.

What does this mean for your visit? A homeopath will appreciate any test results that you bring to the office, but please do not spend too much time talking about them, and certainly spend even less time discussing your conventional medications. Again, a homeopath needs to know about drugs you're taking, but the logic of a conventional physician is not so important to us. Not because it is wrong, but because it is different and cannot become a part of the database. By *database*, I mean the collection of bits of information that will ultimately lead to the selection of a remedy.

Be prepared to describe your food preferences, the position in which you like to sleep, your fears, your dreams, and activities you like to do for fun. A homeopath will spend a lot of time trying to understand what natural things make your symptoms better or worse, such as the time of day, positions, and the temperature. All these bits of information make you different from everyone else experiencing the same complaint.

On any given day, I may see a few patients with migraine headaches and prescribe different remedies for each one of them because of the fact that what triggers their headaches, the precise location of their pain, the things that make them feel better or worse, and the type of personality they each have are different.

On the other hand, I may wind up giving the same remedy to a few people with different diseases. For example, Nancy, a beautiful, shy five-year-old with severe asthma, told me her asthma feels worse inside of the house and always gets better outdoors. Each time she has an asthma attack, she has to sit propped up in bed, becomes tearful, and wants her mommy to hold her and say nice things to her. Her asthma is worse at night. Nancy cries easily and often asks her parents if they love her. She sleeps on her back and always sticks her feet out from under the covers. She cannot stay in the sun because she gets too hot and may even faint. She loves creamy things. Her mother told me that Nancy can eat butter with a spoon. There were many other characteristics I learned in our first visit, and all pointed clearly to a homeopathic remedy named *Pulsatilla nigricans* that cured Nancy's asthma.

A while ago I also saw Jack, a fifty-year-old biker sporting numerous tattoos and a beard. Jack is a big guy. He pumps iron. He likes to wear leather and chains, and he talks in a deep voice. He visited a urologist, complaining of frequent urination. The urologist diagnosed him with prostatitis (an inflammation of the prostate) and prescribed antibiotics. However, a few courses of antibiotics brought about only temporary relief.

Interestingly, this big guy came to see me in the company of his wife of thirty years. During the interview I quickly discovered that this menacing-looking man is actually pretty tender, loves to spend time with his wife, and adores his three daughters. Every time he doesn't feel well, he needs his wife to hold him and tell him how much she loves him. He constantly feels warm and needs the air conditioning to blast all summer. Unfortunately, this creates problems for his wife, who is exactly the opposite. Jack sleeps on his back and always kicks the covers off. He cannot stay out in the sun because it gives him headaches. His frequent urination problem is worse at night. He loves to eat butter and strawberries with a lot of cream.

As I did with little Nancy, I gave Jack *Pulsatilla nigricans* with excellent results.

Interestingly, another two people who love butter, are warm-blooded, or cry easily but otherwise have totally different characteristics would need different remedies. The same is true for their illnesses. Not everyone with asthma needs *Pulsatilla nigricans*, and men with prostate problems require all different kinds of remedies. The unique combination of all the person's symptoms—not just one thing—is the key to finding the remedy.

What Tools Do Homeopaths Use?

You will notice that most contemporary homeopaths use computers. How does this help us find a remedy? Professional homeopathic software contains two main types of books. *Materia Medica*, the Latin title for a book on pharmacology, as discussed in Chapter 2, contains detailed information about each remedy. Another type of book is a repertory. There are many different ones. Each is an index of all the possible symptoms that have been registered by homeopaths, either in provings or from being cured, during use of a particular remedy.

Both types of books compile a massive database that, before the computer age, had to be studied by hand. As modern programs offer searchable libraries equivalent to hundreds of thick books, the computer allows us to handle our searches more efficiently. What the computer cannot do, however, is find a remedy for you. I refer to a good British edition of the main repertory by American homeopath James Tyler Kent so often that the book has lost its front cover. My copy of the currently popular repertory *Synthesis*, edited by F. Shroyens, now also shows clear indications of wear. Identifying and cross-referencing noteworthy symptoms and choosing remedies remain important skills that each homeopath has to gain from many years of continuous study and clinical experience.

Don't be fooled by websites that promise an easy way to find the remedy you need. Also don't be fooled by methods whereby a computer is directly "hooked" to a patient and allegedly measures some kind of a biological field or diagnoses Chinese meridians and finds the remedy based on that. As yet, no reliable correlation has been made between Chinese medicine and homeopathy. Another consideration is that these types of software always seem to come up with a huge list of different supplements, herbs, and various homeopathic preparations that a single person should take. Well, here we go again! That's prescribing multiple medications having unknown interactions with each other and an individual's body. If it still sounds like a good idea, go for it! Clearly, I have my doubts.

Finding a Good Homeopath

The time has come to answer the million-dollar question: how does someone like you find a good homeopath? My answer is not complicated. Basically, you only have two good choices. The first and best option is to go to a homeopath recommended by a friend who has had a good experience with this particular practitioner. Seek satisfied customers. The second option is to consult one of the field's professional organizations.

Let's discuss these associations and schools and their degrees and accreditations.

Different countries have unique regulations about the practice of homeopathy. In some countries, like France, Italy, Russia, India, and a few nations in South America, only highly trained medical professionals can practice homeopathy. In France, Italy, and Russia, only physicians are allowed to practice. India has more than 200,000 homeopathic doctors, and my understanding is that there are two levels of training and degrees, one equal to an M.D. and the other on a par with a physician's assistant (P.A.).

England and Germany have specialized education and licensing for homeopaths: a person is permitted to be a physician and also practice homeopathy. Many industrialized countries—for example, England, France, and Germany—have integrated homeopathy into their national health system. Personally, I am familiar with claim forms that German and French patients ask me to sign to receive full reimbursement for homeopathic services.

The situation in the United States is more complicated. At the time of this writing, only three states—Arizona, Connecticut, and Nevada—license homeopathic practitioners. In Connecticut homeopaths have to be M.D.s and sit for a multiple-choice exam. For a passing score they are granted the title homeopathic physician. In Arizona and Nevada both M.D.s and M.D.-supervised non-M.D.s are permitted to practice homeopathy. Many states recognize naturopathic doctors (N.D.s) as practicing medicine legally, and some N.D.s (but far from all of them!) practice homeopathy. Other states do not explicitly prohibit homeopathy, yet they do not provide a specific certification process.

A recent movement for the freedom of choice in medical treatment has created legislative measures in some states that allow anyone to practice homeopathy. Homeopathic training is provided either by some naturopathic schools as a part of a larger comprehensive curriculum or by independent privately run part-time homeopathic schools. These schools accept students from any background, including M.D.s, N.D.s, nurse practitioners, chiropractors, acupuncturists, and laypeople.

Most medical doctors who practice homeopathy belong to the American Institute of Homeopathy (AIH), which in 1844 was the first professional medical organization established in the United States. Naturopathic doctors likewise have their own organization, the Homeopathic Academy of Naturopathic Physicians (HANP), which was established in 1982. The North American Society of Homeopaths (NASH) was founded in 1990 with a membership that's a mixture of nonlicensed practitioners (the majority) and licensed practitioners. Members of this organization call themselves professional homeopaths, but, as you learned already, their training actually does not differ from that of members from other organizations.

There are three major homeopathic boards in the United States. The American Board of Homeotherapeutics (ABHt) was established by the AIH in 1959. A board of the HANP was established in the 1980s. The Council for Homeopathic Certification (CHC) was created in 1991 to establish a "certification of competency in homeopathy." As of today, none of these certifications provide a license to practice homeopathy. Although there is an ongoing effort to provide a unified certification process, at the moment the ABHt continues to use its own format. All the certification organizations offer a four-part process that includes the review of credentials and training, review of records of about ten cured cases, a written multiple-choice exam, and an oral exam. The process is entirely voluntary, expensive, and laborious. I went through the ABHt certification process myself, and I have to report that it was the most difficult exam I ever took in my life.

The current board of directors of a large organization called the National Center for Homeopathy (NCH) has been working in accord with all the other homeopathic organizations in the United States to provide a climate conducive to collaboration and, ultimately, to better standards of homeopathic care. There is also an ongoing effort to create a full-time fully accredited homeopathic medical school in Arizona.

The Council on Homeopathic Education (CHE) was established in 1982 as an independent agency to assess homeopathic training in the United States and Canada. It has become significantly more active in recent years. Homeopaths have great hopes that its relentless activity will result in a significant improvement in the quality of homeopathic education. The number of schools accredited by CHE is rapidly growing.

In my opinion, claims by the members of one organization or another that their level of proficiency in homeopathy is higher than members of other organizations are subjective. At the end of the day, you, the consumer, are left with the freedom to choose anyone you believe suits your particular situation. I don't feel qualified to endorse or denounce any type of practitioners. The choice ultimately remains yours.

Each of the organizations just mentioned has a website that offers detailed information on the organization's guiding principles and individual practitioners. (See Resources.)

As you read on in *Easy Homeopathy*, you'll be given the opportunity to choose from among seven main remedies and dozens of secondary remedies when you're confronting different emerging and everyday health challenges. If you ever feel confused when making your decision about what remedy to apply, it is perfectly OK—and perhaps even advisable—to seek the counsel of a trained homeopath. I think you'll find, however, that the information in this book is remarkably usable. In due course, you'll become familiar with the seven main remedies and understand their roles in your daily life.

THE SEVEN REMEDIES THAT SHOULD BE IN EVERY MEDICINE CABINET

FOCUS POINTS

Sudden, intense onset ❈ Severe anxiety and fear ❈ Frequently, a fear of imminent death ❈ Restlessness ❈ High fever ❈ Severe thirst

Aconitum

Your Homeopathic Emergency Services Unit

Excessive fear is always powerless.

—AESCHYLUS

ACONITUM NAPELLUS (*Aconite*, monkshood, wolfsbane) leads my descriptions of the seven individual remedies because not only is its name earliest in the alphabet but it also represents the first line of homeopathic defense against a set of serious symptoms. Hopefully, you and your family will never need it. But if you do, it's incredibly valuable.

We use *Aconitum* similarly to the way an emergency services unit responds immediately to the scene of a crisis. This remedy is used to treat the initial stages of a head cold, the flu, or any other acute illness that's characterized by a sudden onset of symptoms and accompanied by fear and restlessness. Children in the earliest stage of

51

croup, for instance, may become extremely frightened and agitated as their throats narrow. *Aconitum* is also used to treat the sort of intense terror and restless anxiety—to the degree of fearing imminent death—that often arise after a person experiences or directly witnesses a horrific event, such as a terrible car crash, a murder, an act of terrorism, or another form of violent crime.

The Origins of *Aconitum*

Aconitum napellus is an impressive plant. Roughly four to five feet tall and decorated with a thick bunch of dark blue blossoms arranged in a spike, the plant usually grows in damp, shady spots in the mountains and flowers during the peak of summer. Since the shape of the flowers is reminiscent of a hood thrown over the head of a monk, the plant is commonly called monkshood.

In Sanskrit, an ancient tongue of Asia, the plant is called by the names Ativisha and Visha. Both words mean "poison." The word *aconite* is derived from the ancient Greek word *akon* (meaning "dart"), which refers to arrows poisoned with the juices of the plant. Wolfsbane refers to its early use as poison bait for wolves. In the Middle Ages, *Aconite* was even believed to protect against werewolves. In some cultures long ago, women were known to use the plant's extracts to poison their unfaithful husbands.

While a homeopathic preparation of *Aconite* is harmless and can cure many cases of severe illness, being poisoned with the plant or its juices produces terrible symptoms. As the root of the plant closely resembles horseradish, in the remote past accidental poisonings with the root were relatively common. The plant was also a popular source of poison for political intrigues. Even before conducting a proving, Dr. Hahnemann already knew many of the symptoms *Aconite* would produce simply because they had been described in literature for many years.

Dr. John Henry Clarke, a renowned British homeopath, once said, "*Aconite* is one of the deadliest and most readily acting poisons, yet, through Hahnemann's discoveries, it has been transformed into the best friend of the nursery." He was referring to the remedy's success in treating croup.

For a poison to be truly effective, it has to produce symptoms quickly, and those symptoms have to be intense enough to lead to death. This is especially true for poisons used in hunting or combat situations. Certainly, plotting the murder of a rival, whether political or romantic, includes an expectation of tremendous suffering by the victim before he or she dies. *Aconite* poisoning fits this profile perfectly. Its symptoms come on suddenly and with great intensity. The victim experiences tremendous anxiety, violent fear, and restlessness. The face feels very hot and there is tremendous thirst. Victims of such symptoms die from respiratory and cardiac arrest.

Symptoms Characteristic of the *Aconitum* State

The symptoms of poisoning lead us in identifying the symptoms characteristic to people who benefit from taking *Aconitum* as a remedy. As you can clearly see, all the reactions are fairly violent, intense, and sudden. The famous American homeopath James Tyler Kent described the picture of an *Aconitum* state in the following way: "All these . . . conditions are attended with great excitement of the circulation, violent action of the heart, a tremendous turmoil of the brain, a violent shock with intense fear."

Any condition that begins with the following unique combination of symptoms can be helped with *Aconitum*:

* ❋ Sudden onset
* ❋ Shock
* ❋ Fright
* ❋ Fear, especially fear of death (usually for no reason)
* ❋ Restlessness
* ❋ Chill or very high fever
* ❋ Tremendous thirst
* ❋ Symptoms that frequently begin after exposure to chilling wind

Circumstances that trigger this combination of symptoms may include the following:

❊ Any acute condition accompanied by both severe fear (especially of imminent death) and restless anxiety
❊ The very beginning of colds, flu, and croup, particularly when the onset is sudden and violent and results in fear and agitation
❊ Being a victim of, or witnessing, a horrific event (interestingly, an event that provokes this state can be described as a chilling experience)

Aconitum states are usually brief. They're experienced and witnessed by relatives and bystanders in the first few minutes or hours after an event occurs or an acute illness sets in. After that, depending on how severe the reaction has been, they can either go away on their own (rare without homeopathy) or they can become worse—possibly leading to a more significant illness that requires treatment with heroic measures to save the person.

Common Colds and Flu

With rare exceptions, *Aconitum* is usually indicated sometime within the first few hours at the beginning of a severe head cold or flu. So unless you get a chance to see a homeopath right away, you're going to need to take this remedy at home. After the initial stage is over, symptoms usually change and people therefore require a different remedy.

An additional clue that *Aconitum* is indicated is that people who need it commonly begin to feel worse late in the evening (twilight or later). On several occasions, I've had to give *Aconitum* to my two children or the children of our neighbors at night, such as in the following case involving one of my daughters.

It was a nice, crispy cold November morning that was a bit on the windy side. My wife, our two children, and I went to see the Macy's Thanksgiving Day Parade, and then we took a stroll around midtown Manhattan. Our children were dressed relatively well for the weather; however, they took their hats off in the middle of our walk, insisting, for some reason, that wearing a winter hat was "not cool" (an interesting choice of words in such cold weather). The rest of the day was pleasant. We came home, had dinner, and went to sleep early.

Around 11 P.M. our elder daughter came to our bed saying that she felt very, very scared. She was shaking from chills. Soon after that, she developed a high fever and became increasingly frightened, anxious, and restless—all uncharacteristic for her. She said, "I've never been so scared in my life," yet she couldn't explain why.

In order to make sure that I wasn't confusing my daughter's state with one that requires *Belladonna* (see Chapter 6), I touched her head and hands and looked into her eyes. Her entire body was hot, and her pupils were small, reflecting sheer horror. She kept asking for additional glasses of cold water. If she had needed *Belladonna*, her hands and/or feet would have been cold. Her pupils would have been so enlarged that she'd have looked as if she'd been drugged. Basically, she would look delirious, rather than agitated. Although she might have reported being scared, she wouldn't have been as restless as she was, and any fear would probably be linked to a scary dream or being afraid of the dark—in other words, there would be some reason for it.

Now I knew! I gave my daughter a dose of three pellets of *Aconitum* 30C. She calmed down in five minutes or so and went to sleep in another five to ten minutes. That was it! In the morning, she was completely recovered.

A skeptic might argue that my daughter would have gotten better anyway. But without homeopathy I don't believe her symptoms would have resolved as quickly as they did. If she'd recovered spontaneously, it's also unlikely there would have been no remnants of the previous night's symptoms whatsoever, as was the case after administering *Aconitum*.

How is homeopathy better than Tylenol in such cases? After all, when you give a child a dose of Tylenol, his fever goes down and the child goes to sleep.

First, remember that you can always give someone Tylenol to suppress the symptoms of an illness after trying a homeopathic remedy. So if the homeopathic remedy doesn't work, you still have another

option. However, it is preferable to encourage the body's own sophisticated defense mechanisms to fight. If homeopathy does help someone improve, it means that person has done it on his own, and his
immune system is being made stronger. A small dose of a natural substance does not mask symptoms.

Secondly, homeopathy produces no side effects. Interestingly,
when high fevers are suppressed quickly with conventional medications, illness can continue to develop and the situation may become
more serious despite (or due to) the lack of a general reaction. Fever
serves a purpose in combating different illnesses.

Spending ten to fifteen minutes or less deciding on a remedy and
another half an hour—maximum—waiting for the remedy you've
chosen to work may save you and your family a lot of trouble and complications. But certainly, when you're in doubt, you should always
consult your physician or, if necessary, call 911. Giving *Aconitum* to
someone who is suffering on the way to the emergency room or doctor's office can make a dramatic difference in that person's life. If you,
your child, or another family member improves after taking the remedy and therefore doesn't require dramatic, heroic treatments in the
end, everybody will be happy.

Reminder: Aconitum is most frequently indicated at the first onset
of an acute illness. Because of this, if symptoms arise at night and you
wait until the morning to select a remedy, you should probably use
another remedy instead of *Aconitum*.

During the final stages of writing this book, the issue of avian flu
became a significant topic in the news. The flu pandemic of 1918,
which took millions of lives on several continents, is still remembered
by the media as if it happened just yesterday. Homeopathic treatment
of the flu provided impressive results during that pandemic, and it
always has. Before we discuss the most commonly used homeopathic
remedies for individualized treatment, let's talk about two popular
homeopathic products marketed for colds and flu: Oscillococcinum
and Influenzinum. Both are used in an allopathic manner: the same
remedy is recommended for everyone without individualization of
treatment. Some research studies and certainly the experience of
thousands of people have proven them effective. If you like simple

solutions, you may try them first before using your brainpower to choose an individual remedy. In many cases, they do the job just fine.

❋ **Oscillococcinum.** The number one over-the-counter flu medication in France, it is also popular in other European countries and is growing in popularity in the United States. It should be used at the first sign of a cold or flu. Instructions are easy to follow and printed on the package. Some people swear by it, others don't find it effective.[1]

❋ **Influenzinum.** This remedy is a homeopathic preparation of the current flu vaccine, manufactured in 9C potency. Like Oscillococcinum, it's popular for flu prevention in Europe, where it is marketed as an alternative to the flu shot for people age two and up. There isn't much scientific evidence of its efficacy, however. According to a ten-year study done in collaboration with twenty-three French homeopathic doctors, it has been effective in 90 percent of cases.[2] I am not familiar with the design of the research study. All I can say is that these numbers seem too optimistic. Yet I have spoken to a number of patients and homeopaths from different countries, and the majority of them swear by this remedy.

Various homeopathic companies sell Influenzinum under different brand names as well as under its generic name. The instructions are the same for all these products. It is recommended to dissolve one dose (the entire contents of a tube) under the tongue each week for four weeks. Then wait for another three weeks before dissolving the contents of one final tube under the tongue.

Let's briefly consider five other frequently indicated and easy-to-distinguish remedies.

Arsenicum album (arsenic trioxide). This remedy is used to treat influenza and colds that include symptoms of gastroenteritis, vomiting, and diarrhea. Gastrointestinal complaints are usually prominent.

Note: unlike *Aconitum*, *Arsenicum* is indicated when there is a period of prodrome, or a gradual onset of symptoms.

Characteristic symptoms:

* High fever (up to 104 degrees) after a few-day onset, perhaps followed by a chill
* Hot face and craving for open air and cold applications to head and face, yet the body is chilled and feels better from warmth
* Thirst for small sips of water (compare with *Bryonia*)
* Significant restlessness with weakness and a tendency to collapse
* Significant anxiety with fear of dying from this illness and desire for company at all times (compare with *Bryonia*)
* Worse: at midnight or 1 A.M. and at noon or 1 P.M.

Belladonna (**deadly nightshade**). This remedy is used for any type of acute illness (including colds and flu) that has a rapid onset and extremely high fever, especially if it's accompanied by a delirious state. *Belladonna* is a commonly indicated remedy for children with a high fever. The key indicator for *Belladonna* is a combination of a confused mental state with a flushed red face that's hot to touch, while hands and/or feet are cold.

Characteristic symptoms (also see Chapter 6):

* Almost delirious with possible hallucinations
* Very high fever (up to 105 degrees)
* Flushed face
* Dilated pupils
* Craving for lemons and, frequently, lemonade
* Frequently, severe, right-sided headache (compare with *Bryonia*)
* Pounding headache (patient feels better in a dark, quiet room)
* Frequently, right-sided sore throat or eye pain
* Worse: frequently aggravated at 3 P.M.

Bryonia alba (**white bryony**). This remedy is used for slowly progressing influenza and common colds in which muscular aching is one of the important symptoms. The key indication is the desire to be absolutely still, as the patient feels much worse from the slightest movement. The patient does everything possible to conserve energy.

Characteristic symptoms:

❁ Internal restlessness but with no tolerance for even the slightest motion
❁ Desire to be left alone, doesn't want to answer questions, irritability without expressing it aloud (compare with *Arsenicum*)
❁ Fever with the pronounced sensation of heat and profuse perspiration
❁ Chills that begin distally (fingertips, toes, rarely the lips) and can be triggered by anger
❁ Great thirst for large gulps at intervals (compare with *Arsenicum*)
❁ Severe headaches located on the front left side of the head or on the back of the head
❁ Worse symptoms generally on the right side of the body (except for the headache, which is on the left)
❁ Usually warm—worse in warm rooms
❁ Worse: frequently at 9 P.M. and from the slightest motion

Eupatorium perfoliatum (boneset). This remedy is used for influenza that includes severe, unbearable aching. The key indicator is a terrible pain that feels as if the bones could break open.
Characteristic symptoms:

❁ High fever (usually above 102 degrees)
❁ Severe, unbearable aching
❁ Chills that begin in the area of the lower back and spread up the spine
❁ Chills that are worse after drinking
❁ Very chilly feeling and sensitivity to cold air
❁ Thirst for cold drinks despite the chill (and frequently during the chill)
❁ Desire for cold food and ice cream
❁ Restlessness from the pain, but motion does not ameliorate symptoms
❁ Worse: from 7 to 9 A.M.

Table 4.1 Common Colds and Flu Remedy Comparison Chart

Remedy	Onset	Better	Worse
Aconitum	Sudden	Open air	Exposure to cold air, warm room; evening and night, after midnight
Belladonna	Sudden	Lemonade; lemons	Afternoon, especially 3 P.M.
Arsenicum	Gradual	Company	Midnight or 1 P.M.
Bryonia	Slow progression	Being alone	Slightest movement; 9 P.M.
Eupatorium	Usually acute	Rest	Cold air; drinking (chills get worse); 7 to 9 A.M.
Gelsemium	Slow, over one to three days	Rest	Motion; 10 A.M.

Gelsemium sempervirens (yellow jasmine). This remedy is used for illness characterized by marked debility, weakness, and sleepiness. The onset is slow, lasting at least twenty-four hours to a few days. The

Emotional State	Signs Guiding Your Selection	Reasons to Say No to This Remedy
Fearful; anxious; restless; children clingy with parents from fear	The very beginning of the illness; no discharges; small pupils; thirst for cold water; high fever and/or chills	Any discharge; late stages (more then a few hours) of illness; absence of fear or anxiety
Confused, possibly hallucinational; possibly appearing sedated	Flushed face; cold hands and feet; dilated pupils; no thirst; frequently, right-sided pounding headache	Small pupils; low-grade fever; significant thirst; discharges; late stages (more than 24 hours) of illness
Very anxious; frequently afraid to die from the illness	Hot face with the rest of the body being very cold; thirst for small sips of water; restlessness with weakness; frequently, diarrhea.	Sudden onset; refuses company; thirst for very large amount of water
Wants to be left alone; refuses to answer questions; irritable	Tremendous thirst; fever with the sensation of heat and profuse perspiration; chills beginning from the fingertips and toes	Communicative; no thirst
Desperate and moaning from pain	Severe, unbearable aching; chills beginning in the lumbar region and spreading up the spine; desire for cold food and drinks	No bone pains; no high fever; no chills
Very sleepy; depressed	Very heavy head, especially in the back; tremendous weakness with heaviness of the limbs and eyelids	Sudden onset; lack of weakness

key indicators are a heavy head as well as heavy eyelids and extremities and pronounced weakness with trembling.

Characteristic symptoms (also see Chapter 8):

* Very heavy head, especially the back of the head
* Chills that run up and down the spine
* Chills that alternate with heat flushes
* Chills accompanied by fine tremors
* Minimal thirst
* Extreme sleepiness
* Eyelids that are half shut or droopy
* Feeling of being somewhat depressed and of dullness
* Worse: aggravation at 10 A.M.

Croup

Croup, the inflammation and narrowing of the air passages, is a potentially life-threatening early childhood illness that should be taken seriously by parents and guardians. Giving a child *Aconitum* can be a life-saving measure, as the following case (which took place more than fifty years ago) perfectly illustrates.

On a cold, dry, windy winter day, when young Wayne was just under a year old, his parents took him out for a walk. That night he woke up screaming. He had a high fever. His face was red when he was lying down but turned pale when his parents picked him up. He also had a scary barking cough, and his breathing was shallow. Each inhalation made him cough and suffocate even more. Drinking liquids made the cough worse. Wayne clung to his mother in fear.

Quickly realizing that their son had croup, his parents decided to go see an old German doctor who lived next door. The parents had known this kindly gentleman for many years and trusted his judgment. But still his treatment seemed bizarre. The doctor examined Wayne, asked them some questions, and then gave their son a single pill. One little pill for a life-threatening situation? Seeing their concerned disbelief, the doctor asked them to wait patiently for a few minutes. Very quickly, in a matter of minutes, Wayne calmed down. Gradually, his breathing became deeper. They took him home and put him to bed. He fell asleep in a matter of fifteen or twenty minutes more. When he woke up again a few hours later with a high fever, another little pill helped him to go back to sleep. In the morning Wayne was fine.

The German doctor was practicing homeopathy, so he knew to give Wayne *Aconitum* 30C in the early stage of croup. Wayne grew up to become a well-known integrative physician and today is one of my colleagues. He incorporates homeopathy in his medical practice. But he rarely sees cases of croup that require *Aconitum* for a simple reason: *Aconitum* is indicated in the first day, or even the first hour, of an attack. It should be given right at the onset, to stop the terror, on the way to the emergency room. Within a couple of hours, an untreated child would need another remedy.

We are living in the twenty-first century. Most families do not live next door to a homeopathic doctor—unless you're one of my neighbors. So parents must become familiar with signs indicating the need for *Aconitum* or a different remedy.

Characteristic indicators for *Aconitum* include:

* Sudden onset, often beginning after exposure to cold, most frequently to a combination of dry cold and wind
* Fear and restlessness
* Awakening from the first part of sleep with a dry, barking, suffocating cough
* Stridor, a shrill wheezing or grunting noise made because of difficulty breathing due to narrowing of the windpipe
* No mucus present
* Clinginess (child to parents)
* Worse: after each inhalation and also when drinking (compare with *Spongia tosta*)

It's also worth mentioning that children who require *Aconitum* for croup are usually robust, which is partly why they develop strong reactions to infections that include lots of heat and movement.

Following are two additional homeopathic remedies for croup.

Spongia tosta (toasted sponge). This is probably the most frequently indicated remedy in the later stages (more than twenty-four hours after the onset) of croup. Essentially, if you don't see characteristic symptoms indicating *Aconitum*, *Spongia tosta* should be your second choice.

Characteristic symptoms:

* Dry, barking cough reminiscent of the sound of a saw going through wood (some authors describe it as a seal's bark)
* Stridor (narrowing of the airways) with noisy, whistling sounds
* Better: after warm drinks or warm food; while eating, drinking, or nursing; while sitting upright or bent forward; when bending head forward (compare with *Hepar sulphuris calcareum*)
* Worse: at midnight or immediately after; much worse from cold air or cold drinks

Hepar sulphuris calcareum (calcium sulphide). The patient is irritable and touchy, cannot tolerate even minimal discomfort, and might scream at the slightest provocation.

Characteristic symptoms:

Table 4.2 Croup Remedy Comparison Chart

Remedy	Onset	Better	Worse
Aconitum	Sudden	Open air	Each inhalation; warm room; evening and night, after midnight
Spongia	After *Aconitum*	Drinking or eating warm things; nursing; bending head forward; sitting upright	Cold drinks; talking; swallowing
Hepar sulphuris	After *Aconitum* and *Spongia*	Throwing head backward; eating	Slightest touch or draft; being uncovered

* Onset frequently between 2 and 4 A.M. or toward morning
* Thick, rattling mucus
* Better: when throwing the head backward (compare with *Spongia tosta*)
* Worse: when being uncovered and becoming even slightly cold

Note: if your child is having difficulty breathing, you should seek immediate medical attention. A remedy (including *Aconitum*) should be given on your way to the emergency room. Don't lose precious time. You and your child are much better off wrong than sorry! In cases of croup, for example, a continuous wheezing breath could be a sign of a more serious problem—epiglottis, which requires immediate professional attention.

Acute Post-Traumatic Stress Disorder

Nelly, a middle-aged woman, requested an immediate appointment after being mugged at gunpoint in the elevator of her apartment building the night before. After this terrorizing experience she had

Emotional State	Signs Guiding Your Selection	Reasons to Say No to This Remedy
Fearful; anxious; restless; children clingy with parents from fear	The very beginning of the illness; loud, difficult breathing; no mucus; high fever and/or chills	Any discharge; late stages (more then a few hours) of illness; absence of fear or anxiety
Anxious	Feeling cold; better from warm drinks; throat sensitive to touch	Worse from warm drinks or food; better from bending head backward
Very irritable and touchy; screams at the slightest provocation	Rattling mucus; very irritable	Better from bending head forward; no mucus

lost sleep. She found herself so scared that she couldn't lie down or even sit still. Thoughts of imminent death kept running through her mind. When one of her friends told Nelly about me, she wasted no time before phoning me. She decided to see whether homeopathy could help her feel better.

The first thing I noticed when Nelly came into my office was an expression of fear on her face. She was terrified beyond an ability to function. A nice, polite person, she attempted to sit on the chair I offered but was unable to remain still. Her legs, arms, and entire torso were continuously moving. I let her know that she didn't have to sit if she couldn't. While moving in circles around my small office, Nelly informed me that she was going to die soon. In fact, she was sure it was going to happen in exactly five days. She just knew it. Our interview was difficult. Nelly was obviously scared and anxious. She couldn't go on like that much longer. I quickly decided on the remedy: *Aconitum*.

Being an experienced homeopath, I felt it was appropriate to give Nelly a dose of 200C. In your own "family practice," I only recommend using remedies in the homeopathic concentration 30C. The exception to this rule of thumb is *Arnica montana* (see Chapter 5).

The effect of the *Aconitum* was amazing. Within three to five minutes after taking the dose, Nelly was able to sit down. We continued our interview. By the time we finished (in another forty-five minutes or so), Nelly felt much better. I didn't give her any more remedies. That was it. For this most terrifying episode of her life, *Aconitum* did the job.

I see a lot of people with emotional problems in my practice, and I feel sorry when I find out that those who are suffering from post-traumatic stress disorder didn't have access to *Aconitum* immediately after a horrifying experience. A significant proportion of people require *Aconitum* under those conditions. My friend Manfred, a homeopath from Germany, sent one kilogram (two pounds) of *Aconitum* to Honduras after a devastating earthquake. He travels there frequently and has been able to witness how much good *Aconitum* can do, when used judiciously.

Certainly, not every single individual who goes through such an experience will need *Aconitum*. Many require another homeopathic remedy. In fact, even individuals who have had a similar experience may exhibit symptoms requiring different treatments. "I couldn't believe it. I woke up and the airplane was sitting in my garage. They even found airplane parts in the bedroom. My enemies should be that lucky!" Jackie told me. She is an eighty-two-year-old widow. Strong. Tough. With no emotional problems before November 12, 2001. That morning, she woke up to a terrible noise. A large part of an airplane that crashed in Belle Harbor, New York, landed in her garage. Jackie and her nephew Sam were both shaken physically and emotionally by the event.

A large number of New York City firefighters live in the neighborhood, so many off-duty firefighters came to the rescue almost immediately, even before those on duty had arrived. Because the crash happened two months after the World Trade Center collapsed, people at first thought it was another attack.

Jackie was terrified. She couldn't sleep without the lights on and had severe night terrors a few times a night. She also couldn't concentrate and felt she needed to have other people around, especially at night. Her nephew had to move into the same room with her to keep her company. He and Jackie's son took turns "babysitting" her around the clock. Previously independent, she became anxious and listless. In a state of anguish, she constantly felt as though she were in danger. The key features of her case were a constant state of fear of impending danger; an inability to concentrate; frequent, vivid night terrors; and a desire for company.

Without going into too much detail, this combination of symptoms points toward another homeopathic remedy, *Stramonium*, one dose of which resolved Jackie's condition in a few weeks. Eventually, Jackie saw me for other problems and responded well to the homeopathic remedies indicated at that time. She is still doing well.

Jackie's nephew Sam, who lived in the house with her, responded differently to the same incident. He kind of froze. He was becoming dreamy, absentminded, and anxious in his sleep, and he started thinking about death. "The weirdest thing, doc, is that I sometimes feel like somebody is lying in my bed with me," he told me. He complained of becoming lazy and indifferent to everything, "even to girls." He also became extremely constipated. All these symptoms were unusual for him. The remedy indicated in Sam's case was *Opium*.

A layperson cannot go out and buy *Opium*. Even though it's extremely diluted in homeopathic formulations, it is still a controlled substance and requires a prescription written by a licensed health care professional registered with the Drug Enforcement Agency (DEA). Sam did well after taking one pill of *Opium* 200C. He rapidly became strong as a rock again and returned to working hard and having fun.

These two examples merely illustrate how differently two individuals may react to a similar situation. It is important for laypeople not to attempt on their own to treat complex situations with homeopathy. It is one thing to take or to give somebody else a clearly indicated remedy in an acute (nonchronic) situation. It is a totally different thing to prescribe a remedy for someone who's been suffering for a while. There are usually many issues involved in chronic conditions.

Internet research has made a vast amount of information available to the general public. Thus many people believe they are capable of determining the appropriate course of treatment. But it is not so. Only a well-trained, professional homeopath with clinical experience is prepared to deal with complicated situations. While *Aconitum* is frequently indicated in the initial stages of an acute illness and may help to abort its progress completely, chronic illnesses or chronic distress require a sophisticated approach and treatments that cannot be learned simply by reading a book or a website or two.

A Few More Conditions That May Require *Aconitum*

There are many scenarios that may trigger *Aconitum* states, from experiencing an earthquake to being trapped in an enclosed space.

A child who gets scared on an airplane and then runs around screaming from terror will generally do well after a dose of *Aconitum*, for example.

Some people are morbidly afraid of dentists. Imagine how wonderful it would be if anyone who feared death from pain could relax after taking a dose of *Aconitum*. Poor dental hygiene is a simple, everyday scenario that can lead to much worse conditions if it's left untreated. Resistant patients put themselves at risk when they avoid dental care. Likewise, a person who's avoiding necessary surgery due to dread and agitation may feel considerable relief from *Aconitum*.

A woman about to undergo a difficult labor who is feeling total panic and agitation could benefit from taking this remedy. So could a woman who has already given birth to a baby and is now bleeding, if her condition is accompanied by a tremendous fear of death, anxiety, and agitation.

Note: while *Aconitum* is generally safe for pregnant women and infants, if you are pregnant or nursing it is recommended that you consult with a professional homeopath on the appropriate dosage before taking any remedies.

A person who just sustained a significant physical injury and now feels restless and scared that he or she is going to die could also do well after the administration of *Aconitum*.

The list of possible triggers mentioned here is only a guideline. Remember that homeopathy is used to treat individuals rather than specific illnesses or conditions.

FOCUS POINTS

Severe trauma after blows and falls ❀ Concussion of the brain ❀
Shock after injury ❀ Sore, bruised, beaten-up feeling ❀ Denies need
for help ❀ Fear after accidents

 **5**

Arnica
Your Homeopathic Surgeon

*Children show scars like medals. Lovers use
them as secrets to reveal.*

— LEONARD COHEN

THE HEALING properties of *Arnica montana* (leopard's bane), the
second in our growing collection of outstanding remedies, have
been recognized for millennia. Well known to the ancient Greeks and
Romans for its medicinal powers to heal wounds and falls, the plant
in antiquity was called *Panacea laprosum*, literally meaning, "cure
for falls." As you can see from this brief history, *Arnica*—even the
nonhomeopathic herb—has long been celebrated as a remedy par
excellence for the treatment of injuries.

Dr. Hahnemann already possessed many good sources of information when he decided to conduct provings of this important plant.
His research confirmed the herb's amazing curative properties and

71

revealed many characteristics unique to patients needing *Arnica*. Interestingly, the majority of victims of the kind of trauma where the major impact is on the muscles and bones develop symptoms calling for this seemingly magical remedy. In his description of *Arnica*, Hahnemann wrote, "The symptoms of all injuries caused by severe contusions and lacerations of the fibers [muscles] are tolerably uniform in character, and . . . these symptoms are contained in striking homoeopathic similarity in the alterations of the health which *Arnica* develops in the healthy human subject."[1]

This chapter will explore the uses of *Arnica* and other remedies beneficial for treating general injuries and trauma, postoperative recovery, bites and insect stings, burns, near drowning, and fainting. As you'll discover, *Arnica* is an incredibly valuable item to keep stocked in your home medicine cabinet.

The Origins of *Arnica*

Leopard's bane, the folk name for our herb, reflects the similarity of its bright yellow flowers to the eyes of a wildcat. The name *Arnica* is derived from the Greek word for lamb, *arnos*, which refers to the similarity in texture of its leaves and flowers to the soft fur of the farm animal. *Montana* (Latin for mountain) signals that the plant grows at high altitudes.

Mountain dwellers understood the therapeutic qualities of the herb, which conveniently grows in the mountains of Germany, Switzerland, and Siberia, and they used its infusion to cure ailments related to falls and head trauma. (An infusion is a solution made by steeping an herb in water.) Legend has it that in olden times mountain climbers chewed fresh leaves from the plant to ease the soreness of their muscles and to help their bruises heal faster. But as we know today, raw *Arnica* is poisonous.

Warning: You should never ingest the *Arnica* plant itself. Only homeopathically prepared *Arnica* is safe for consumption.

In German folk medicine *Arnica* was called *Fallkraut* (fall plant). The illustrious German nun Hildegard of Bingen—a visionary, composer, and accomplished naturalist and herbal healer beatified by the

Catholic Church—wrote extensively about the properties of *Arnica* in the beginning of the twelfth century.[2]

Homeopathic *Arnica montana* is prepared from the whole fresh plant when it is in bloom. Its preparations have been successfully used for the effective and extremely prompt treatment of both severe and mild injuries and in the prevention of complications from surgery. That's why *Arnica* is a cornerstone of homeopathic first aid. If you could remember only a single homeopathic remedy, *Arnica* would be that remedy, as it helps so many children and adults avoid potential complications of severe trauma. It saves lives.

In many ways *Arnica* has become a symbol of homeopathy. Most health food stores now carry it in gels and ointments, as well as standard pellets. Nearly all parents in large industrial centers know something about *Arnica* and use it to handle everything that comes up in their households, from minor bruises to cases of severe trauma.

Symptoms Characteristic of the *Arnica* State

As has been repeatedly mentioned, *Arnica* is the main remedy indicated in cases of trauma. It is so effective in this regard, in fact, that some homeopathic authors have compared similarly valuable remedies for other types of conditions to it. For instance, you may read that "*Ignatia* is *Arnica* for the emotions." Although it is true that cases of severe trauma and surgical interventions producing damage to both muscles and superficial bone structures almost always require this remedy, it is also true that there are highly specific emotional symptoms and modalities that pinpoint the need (or lack thereof) for *Arnica*. As you'll recall, a modality is something that makes a condition better or worse.[3]

If you or someone else in your family is exhibiting the correct physical, mental, and emotional indicators, *Arnica* is the remedy for the condition you are treating. If not, then taking another remedy is more appropriate.

Once you've identified that it is the appropriate remedy, *Arnica* must be administered in a particular dose and following a particular schedule. Mindless use of *Arnica* for minor bruises or unnecessary repetitions of *Arnica* before and after surgery may lead someone who consumes it to experience certain complications, such as bruising. As you already understand from reading Chapter 2 (see "Less Is More: The Principle of Minimal Dose"), too frequent administration of a single homeopathic remedy can exacerbate your symptoms for the same reasons that the remedy could cause a proving in a healthy, sensitive individual. Later in this chapter, I'll give you detailed instructions for administering *Arnica*.

The most characteristic symptoms of the *Arnica* state are as follows:

❀ Sore, bruised feeling
❀ Feeling beaten, either in the entire body or in the affected part
❀ Restless in bed because it feels too hard
❀ Shock after injury (patient often denies needing help or that anything is wrong)
❀ Fear after accidents
❀ Bleeding (for example, a nosebleed) after washing the face (renowned American homeopath Paul Herscu has described how he used *Arnica* to cure a pregnant woman who developed uterine bleeding after washing her face)

Things that improve the condition include the following:

❀ Lying down with head low
❀ Cold applications
❀ Open air
❀ Changing position

Things that make the condition worse include the following:

❀ Touch
❀ Heat
❀ Rest on one side or being in one position for too long
❀ Nighttime, after sleep

The following circumstances often require using *Arnica* as the first choice:

❖ Any severe accident that would require you to call 911
❖ Trauma: injuries of soft tissues (skin plus muscle), such as injuries from blows, falls, or strikes from blunt objects
❖ Concussion of the brain (after jarring head injuries or motor vehicle accidents), subtle symptoms of which include headache, dizziness, personality changes, memory loss, or feelings of being foggy, distracted, or fatigued
❖ Bleeding caused by injury
❖ Shock from injury
❖ Fear after injury
❖ Soreness after tooth extraction or dental surgery
❖ Dental or other surgery when there is going to be damage to skin, muscle, or bone—for example, during wisdom tooth extraction or any other serious dental surgery, orthopedic surgery, facial plastic surgery, breast augmentation, or mastectomy (*Arnica* should be taken prophylactically prior to the procedure)

Injuries and Trauma

The rule of thumb is the sooner you give *Arnica*, the better. Personally, I always carry *Arnica montana* 10M in the glove compartment of my car in case I happen to pass a serious motor vehicle accident along the road I'm driving.

In an emergency, give an accident victim three pellets of *Arnica montana* 200C (or 1M, 10M, or 50M) on the way to the emergency room. Usually these doses are sufficient for moderate to serious injuries. For minor injuries, or if you do not have any other potency on hand, you can use 30C tablets. Give the accident victim three pellets under the tongue right away, and follow with two to three more doses at fifteen- to thirty-minute intervals.

Here are a couple additional principles to keep in mind:

❖ The more severe an injury is, the higher the potency of *Arnica* you should use, and the less time there should be between repetitions.

❋ The only time you should exceed three repetitions is when the trauma is severe but only *Arnica montana* 30C is available. In that case, you should repeat the dose every fifteen minutes for up to five times.

Hahnemann suggested simultaneous external and internal use of *Arnica* in cases where there is damage to the skin and/or muscles. For minor injuries, such as superficial bruises and bumps, apply an *Arnica* gel or ointment topically on the skin. There is no reason to take *Arnica* pills in such cases, as no actual damage to the rest of the person (the mind, the emotions) has been done. The body of the injured person, especially in the case of a healthy child, should be able to deal with minor problems without unnecessary help. Parents too frequently give their children *Arnica* tablets for minor bruises. This is a mistake, as the use of *Arnica* ointment alone is effective. *Warning:* do not use *Arnica* gel or ointment if the skin is broken, as it is an irritant.

One of my adult patients suffered significant bruising after a car accident. Her family members knew the benefits of *Arnica*, yet they only had *Arnica* ointment on hand. Her sister applied the ointment wherever she could see a bruise already developing. Interestingly, in a few days the treated areas had no bruising, while the areas that were ignored, because they originally had no obvious bruising, turned black and blue. In this situation, *Arnica montana* 200C tablets would also have been appropriate.

I can recall plenty of situations where *Arnica* was clearly indicated and prevented extremely serious complications. The two that follow involved experienced homeopaths.

In the first case, a well-known homeopathic teacher was walking back into the classroom after a break. Because he was thoroughly engaged in an animated conversation with one of his students, he walked into the door frame at a pretty good speed. The impact was significant. The man almost fell and looked confused for a brief moment. Quickly he then stated, "I'm OK, guys. I need no help." Even before the end of this phrase, the entire class and the teacher himself started to laugh. We all recognized his statement as one of the main characteristics of the *Arnica* state: he believed he was OK despite experiencing a severe blow. Fortunately, a few people in class had homeopathic kits containing *Arnica* with them. The teacher's head and our schedule were both saved.

Another scary scenario unfolded on Alonissos, a beautiful Greek island that is famous in homeopathic circles because it houses the International Academy of Classical Homeopathy, which is run by the world-renowned homeopath George Vithoulkas. I arrived there to conduct a small research study with a large group of experienced homeopaths and was invited for a "safe" boat trip to get to know them. I do get seasick easily, but the promise was made that the sea would be quiet that evening. We would just eat, have a few drinks, watch the stars, and socialize. Such was not the case. A storm set in right in the middle of our trip. I saw the accident happen because I was sitting in the stern of the boat, turning green from nausea and trying to get as much air as I could.

As a wave rocked the boat, one of my fellow homeopaths slipped on the floor and hit the back of his head on a bench. We all heard a scary sound from the impact. A few people surrounded the man. Although he was bleeding, the first words out of his mouth were, "I'm OK, guys. No big deal!" You can be sure he received *Arnica* almost immediately and that the dose was repeated a few times.

To the total surprise and utter disbelief of many medical staffs, on some occasions the victim of a serious accident will arrive at the ER without showing signs of the typical pain and swelling because they've taken a few doses of *Arnica*. Of course, a fracture always requires prompt professional intervention so bones can be set and complications prevented. However, if you take *Arnica*, the amount of pain and swelling accompanying a fracture is usually significantly less than otherwise expected in such a severe case.

Following are eleven other remedies that may be indicated for accident victims. See Table 5.1 starting on page 82 for a comparison chart of the remedies.

Aconitum napellus (monkshood). This remedy is usually indicated in the first moments after a horrific trauma when someone becomes morbidly scared and has severe agitation and restlessness (also see Chapter 4).

❋ Sudden onset
❋ Shock
❋ Fright
❋ Fear, especially fear of death (usually for no reason)
❋ Restlessness
❋ Chill or very high fever
❋ Tremendous thirst

Bellis perennis (common daisy). This remedy is indicated for cases of trauma to internal organs, such as the liver, spleen, or uterus. It is also appropriate if swelling persists for a long time after an injury, despite administering *Arnica* or another appropriate remedy.

Bryonia alba (white bryony). You should seriously consider this remedy whenever trauma to the bones is involved. You can recognize this because the victim will refuse to move.

❋ Severe pain and discomfort made worse by even the slightest motion
❋ Feeling of internal restlessness but no tolerance for even the slightest motion
❋ Desire to be left alone, doesn't want to answer questions, irritability without expressing it aloud
❋ Better: from anything that prevents motion, such as firm pressure or lying on the injured part of the body

Carbo vegetabilis (vegetable charcoal). This remedy is indicated when the victim faints.

❋ Need for constant fanning
❋ Severe weakness
❋ Significant coldness of the injured area

Chamomilla (German chamomile). This remedy is indicated for fainting from severe pain.

✼ Extreme sensitivity to pain
✼ Better and worse: no specific modalities in this situation; the patient just needs *Chamomilla* to get better

Ferrum phosphoricum (phosphate of iron).

✼ Fever after a head injury
✼ Better: from cold applications
✼ Worse: at night and from 4 to 6 A.M., also from touch, jarring, and motion

Hamamelis virginiana (witch hazel). *Instructions:* to increase its action against bruising, try combining *Hamamelis* ointment or gel with an equal amount of *Arnica* ointment. Apply twice a day. Simultaneously, take three 30C pellets.

✼ Severe bruises that swell and bleed (use pellets only)
✼ Nosebleeds that last a long time, even after administering *Arnica* (use pellets only)

Hypericum perforatum (Saint-John's-wort). This remedy is appropriate for trauma to parts of the body abundant with peripheral nerves, such as crushed fingers and toes, as well as spinal injuries.

✼ Possible depression or upset after injury
✼ Better: from rubbing and rest
✼ Worse: from cold, foggy weather, and dampness

Ruta graveolens (garden rue). This remedy is useful for trauma to the periosteum (connective tissue that wraps around the bones), especially in areas where the bone is close to the skin, like the shinbone, the pelvis, and the elbow.

✼ Restlessness because of soreness
✼ Anxiety, irritability, and upset with others

* Better: from continuous, gentle motion
* Worse: from first motion, sitting, and touch

Sanguinaria canadensis (**bloodroot**). This remedy is almost a specific treatment for post-traumatic right shoulder pain. (Sorry—homeopaths don't have a similar remedy yet for the left shoulder.)

Instructions: take three pellets of *Sanguinaria canadensis* 12C once a day for twenty days. Stop taking doses if your pain disappears earlier.

* Irritability in the evening
* Desire to be held and comforted
* Better: from rest and lying down
* Worse: at night and from raising the arm

Symphytum officinale (**comfrey**). This is an excellent remedy for broken bones that don't heal.

Instructions: take five pellets of *Symphytum officinale* 6C three times a day for twenty days—or for fewer days in cases of a speedy recovery.

Surgery, Before and After

As I stated before, giving people too much *Arnica* can cause provings in them. Plastic surgeons and individuals who undergo plastic surgery have known about the benefits of homeopathic *Arnica* for a long time. But some surgeons got so excited about its effects that they suggested their patients take it for two weeks prior to surgery and then take additional postoperative doses. To their surprise, these patients were more bruised after surgery and bled more than normal. These complications clearly resulted from misuse.

There are two correct ways to use *Arnica* when you're having surgery.

* A simple schedule is to take three pellets of *Arnica* 200C right before surgery, three pellets after the surgery is finished (if dental surgery is being done under local anesthesia, ask your dentist to place

three pellets in your mouth) or after you wake up from anesthesia, and three pellets that night before going to sleep.

❀ For people who either don't have time to make the arrangements I just described or prefer their medications to look more real, meaning to resemble conventional drugs, Alpine Pharmaceuticals created a product called SinEcch. The package contains capsules holding various concentrations of *Arnica* along with a schedule of how to take them. Rest assured that this medication is homeopathic *Arnica* only, nothing else. It is easy to take in the form in which it is presented. Thus this preparation is becoming popular with plastic surgeons and their clients.

Following are five remedies that people undergoing surgery often benefit from instead of taking *Arnica*. As you can see, the instructions are very simple and straightforward. Usually the few symptoms listed here will suffice to give you a good idea about which remedy to choose.

Aconitum napellus (monkshood). This remedy is helpful for shock and fright before and after surgery when the person is morbidly scared and, especially, when the person is convinced that he or she will die during the operation.

Instructions: one to two doses of 30C or 200C taken every fifteen minutes can make a huge difference. (Compare with *Gelsemium*.)

Calendula officinalis (marigold). This remedy helps to speed up the healing of surgical wounds without complications.

Instructions: the most efficient way to use *Calendula officinalis* is to take five pellets of 6C three times a day for twenty days and also to apply *Calendula* ointment on the wound (after the surgeon removes the dressing) twice a day.

Gelsemium sempervirens (yellow jasmine). This remedy works well for severe anxiety before surgery. The individual in this state may be trembling with fear and may feel weak. Compare the picture for *Gelsemium* with the *Aconitum* state, where a reaction is strong

Table 5.1 Injuries and Trauma Remedy Comparison Chart

Type of Trauma	Remedy	Better	Worse
The main remedy to consider for any physical trauma	*Arnica*	Cold applications; lying down, especially with head low; changing position	Touch; jarring; drinking wine
Initial stages of any trauma, both physical and emotional	*Aconitum*	No specific factors; generally better in the open air	Lying on the painful side; warm room
Trauma to internal organs (liver, spleen, uterus); swelling that does not go away after *Arnica*	*Bellis*	Continued motion; rest; cold applied locally	Chill and being wet; hot bathing and warmth of bed; before storm
Any acute trauma with typical symptoms, especially trauma to the bones and joints	*Bryonia*	Immobilization of the injured part, from lying on the painful side, a brace, a tight bandage, or pressure; local heat	Any motion, even turning slightly, moving the eyes, or taking a deep breath
Fainting after severe injury	*Carbo vegetabilis*	Desire to be fanned	No modalities related to trauma
Fainting from pain	*Chamomilla*	No specific modalities in this particular case	Severe pain, as perceived by the victim
Fever after head injury	*Ferrum phosphoricum*	Cold applications	At night and 4 to 6 A.M.; touch; jarring; motion
Severe bruises that swell and bleed even after *Arnica*	*Hamamelis*	No modalities related to trauma	No modalities related to trauma

Emotional State	Signs Guiding Your Selection	Reasons to Say No to This Remedy
In shock after injury; convinced that nothing is wrong; sends help away	First remedy for blunt injury, bruising, accidents; thoughts that everything is OK despite sometimes having severe injury; inability to find comfortable position in bed because it feels too hard	In cases of broken skin (open wounds) do not use ointment or tincture
Fearful, anxious, and restless, frequently with fear of imminent death	Extreme fear with restlessness immediately after trauma	Absence of fear, anxiety
No specific mental picture has been described yet	Intense soreness; trauma to internal organs; after *Arnica* failed	Rarely indicated as the first remedy after musculoskeletal trauma (start from *Arnica*)
Very irritable and touchy; screams at the slightest provocation; wants to be alone (due to fear of being touched)	Much worse from motion; trauma to bone structures; does not want to be disturbed	Moves without problems, or with pain, but does not require to be absolutely still
No modalities related to trauma	Desire to be fanned	Fainting from severe pain (instead, give *Chamomilla*); no fainting; no need for constant fanning
No modalities related to trauma	Extreme sensitivity to slightest pain	When symptoms clearly indicate *Carbo vegetabilis*
No modalities related to trauma	Fever after head injury with few or no modalities; no typical modalities for *Arnica* or other remedies described	Lack of fever (in that case, give *Arnica*)
No specific trauma-related symptoms	Large, swollen, bleeding bruises that remain after *Arnica*	No significant bruising prior to use of *Arnica*

continued

Table 5.1 Injuries and Trauma Remedy Comparison Chart *(continued)*

Type of Trauma	Remedy	Better	Worse
Crushed fingers and/ or toes; spinal injury; injury to peripheral nerves	*Hypericum*	Rubbing; rest	Cold; cold foggy weather; dampness
Trauma to tendons; trauma to wrist, shin, knee, ankle	*Ruta*	Continued gentle motion	First motion; sitting; touch
Right-sided post-traumatic shoulder pain	*Sanguinaria*	Rest; lying down	Raising the arm; at night
Fracture; nonunion of bones	*Symphytum*	No specific modalities	No specific modalities

and includes terror and an overwhelming fear of death. (Also see Chapter 8.)

Phosphorus (phosphorus). This remedy helps relieve bad effects of anesthesia, like disorientation, anxiety, nausea, and vomiting. It's helpful for nausea and vomiting after abdominal surgery. The most characteristic symptom in these cases is vomiting immediately after food or drinks warm up in the stomach (usually a few minutes after ingestion).

Staphysagria (Delphinium staphysagria). This remedy helps in cases of trauma and/or pain and even bleeding after urinary catheterizations.

Instructions: take three pellets of *Staphysagria* 30C three times at fifteen-minute intervals on your way to the urologist. In cases where there are complications, you should always consult a physician. Better safe than sorry.

Emotional State	Signs Guiding Your Selection	Reasons to Say No to This Remedy
May be depressed or upset after injury; rarely may report that after injury head feels longer or even lifted in the air	Crushed fingers; trauma to peripheral nerves and spine	No significant trauma to peripheral nerves and/or fingers or toes
Restless because of soreness; anxious; irritable; upset with others	Specific for trauma to the wrist and periosteum	No significant trauma to periosteum or wrist
Irritable in the evening; wants to be held and comforted	Specific for right-sided shoulder trauma (chronic or acute)	Left-sided complaints
No specific modalities	Fractures; nonunion of bones	Bones not yet set by a specialist

Bites and Insect Stings

An animal bite (or human bite) or insect sting can pose an emergency. When you are faced with these kinds of trauma, *Arnica* is a possibility, but it is not the first solution you should consider.

Most often, insect stings and bites don't require any kind of treatment other than cleaning out the wound with soap and water. Hydrogen peroxide is always a good choice, too, as it kills many dangerous bacteria and cleans wounds well. But as they do after their children take minor falls, parents frequently overuse homeopathic remedies in cases of insect bites, even though an uncomplicated sting from one bee usually doesn't require a remedy. The exception is the person allergic to bee stings.

My favorite external application for bee stings is a product called Gold Star balm, which is sold in Chinese and Korean stores. It comes in a cute little red tin container with, as you might imagine, a gold star on it. A single application usually takes the itching and stinging feeling away and reduces localized swelling. If you don't have a balm handy, ice and a little bit of aloe vera would probably solve the problem.

Now if someone has a systemic reaction to an insect bite or sting and/or if the area becomes significantly swollen and painful, a homeopathic remedy can do miracles.

Animal bites and human bites present significant problems, as they get infected quickly and have a tendency to heal slowly with a lot of complications. Homeopathic remedies promote faster healing of such injuries and decrease or sometimes even prevent scar formation. The sooner someone gets the right remedy, the better the outcome will be.

Please don't forget to clean and disinfect bite wounds, too.

Arnica is appropriate for bites whenever you see significant trauma to a combination of skin, muscles, and even a bone. The only other possible situation is a bite by a large dog without any damage done to the skin. Typically for the *Arnica* state, the victim will not consider the situation serious.

Following are other very helpful remedies for different kinds of bites and stings. As you'll notice from the following descriptions, *Arnica* cannot be considered a primary remedy for these conditions. But one can never rule it out entirely.

Aconitum napellus (monkshood). I've seen cases when a child, or even an adult, stung by a bee gets so scared that the need for *Aconitum* is obvious. Use it if someone is scared, is red in the face, and has an expression of terror such that the pupils of the eyes become tiny. One dose of *Aconitum* 30C will resolve this issue, and then you have to wait and see. Taking this remedy may be sufficient, or afterward the victim may also develop symptoms that indicate a need for another remedy (refer to the following).

Apis mellifica (honeybee). Use this remedy if the area of a sting is swollen red and warm to the touch and if the condition is made better by cold. (Compare with the picture of *Ledum*, in which the area is usually cold and reddish blue.) Frequently, the person who needs *Apis* is quite irritable; it's easy for this individual to fly off the handle. I've seen cases of severe allergic reactions to bee stings that almost instantly respond to *Apis*. Severe swelling with inflammation after stings from other insects responds similarly as well.

Instructions: a dose of 30C, either dry or in water (e.g., the plussing method, see Chapter 2), is good. If there's an initial, but not a complete, improvement, repeat the dose two more times at thirty- to sixty-minute intervals. Stop giving doses sooner if the victim is more than 50 percent better.

Don't use *Apis*—or any other remedy, for that matter—just because there's a situation in which it's frequently indicated. The bites of wasps and other large insects often require *Ledum palustre*, but not always. Assess what's going on with the victim for a few minutes before making your selection.

Bites from Snakes, Scorpions, and Spiders

Homeopathy is effective in the treatment of bites by snakes, scorpions, and spiders. It's also effective for treatment of severe allergic reactions to bites and stings. Following are descriptions of a few remedies that can be helpful with these issues. If you're an avid traveler and your family spends time in the wilderness, make sure you have these remedies handy, along with other first-aid items.

Carbolicum acidum (carbolic acid). In this picture the patient has a dusky red face, but the skin around the mouth and nose is pale. The victim also reports a choking feeling and frequently becomes lethargic but, even so, may paradoxically develop an acute awareness of odors. In cases of allergic reactions, someone develops hives over the entire body.

Instructions: give repeated 30C doses every ten to fifteen minutes until improvement or the arrival of the ambulance. You should always call 911 or go to the ER if you see these symptoms develop. If the condition arises during a camping trip, give the remedy and then head toward a populated area as fast as you can!

Lachesis muta (bushmaster snake venom). Dr. Hering discovered this important homeopathic remedy more than a hundred years ago.

Table 5.2 Bites and Insect Stings Remedy Comparison Chart

Type of Trauma	Remedy	Better	Worse
Psychological trauma immediately after the bite or even at the sight of the animal or an insect (humans bite, too)	*Aconitum*	No specific modalities	No specific modalities
Bee and other small insect stings	*Apis*	Cold applications	Heat locally and generally
Wasp and other large insect bites; the remedy of choice for tick bites; the remedy of choice for animal and human bites	*Ledum*	Ice-cold applications	Heat, although the person is chilly; even the slightest touch or pressure
Jellyfish and medusa stings; insect bites and stings	*Urtica urens*	Continuous rubbing	No specific modalities
Severe allergic reaction to bee and other insect stings and bites	*Carbolicum acidum*	No specific modalities	No specific modalities
Poisonous bites by snakes and large spiders	*Lachesis*	No specific modalities	Heat
Severe reactions to snake bites	*Oxalicum acidum*	No specific modalities	Thinking about the problem; touch; light

In cases of poisonous bites by snakes or spiders, it can be beneficial. The affected part has a dusky purple color. Frequently, you'll see a continuous oozing of blood from the wound.

Emotional State	Signs Guiding Your Selection	Reasons to Say No to This Remedy
Fearful (frequently fearful of imminent death); anxious; restless	Extreme fear (including fear of dying); panic; restlessness; immediately after a bite	Absence of fear and anxiety
Irritable; busy	Stinging (like from a bee sting) pain; swelling; redness; area is warm or hot to touch	Absence of swelling with redness and heat
Wants to be alone	Bite area is cold to touch; person is cold but wants ice-cold applications to the wound and won't let go of it; bite area is bluish	Feeling of heat; irritability
No specific modalities	Blotches (urticaria) with violent itching (like from stinging nettles) that gets better from constant rubbing	No blotches
Lethargic	Severe allergic reactions to bee stings (could be to other insects) with dusky face, but skin around mouth and nose is pale; blotches and/or vesicles covering the entire body	Agitation and irritability (think about *Apis*)
Anxious	Dusky purple bite area with oozing blood	No obvious signs to say no
Confused; feels worse thinking about the problem	Numbness; violent pain; trembling	Needs to be rushed to the nearest hospital

Instructions: give a 200C dose once and apply an ice pack to prevent the poison from spreading. Of course, professional help must be on its way or you should be rushing toward the nearest hospital right away!

Ledum palustre (**marsh tea**). This remedy should be considered first for animal bites, including those from dogs, cats, raccoons, and snakes, and human bites, and for the stings and bites of large insects, such as wasps. A main indication is that the area of the bite or sting is reddish blue and surrounded by a very pale area. The wound is also cold to the touch (compare with *Apis mellifica*). This remedy is appropriate for puncture wounds and bites—both human and animal.

Paradoxically, ice-cold applications will bring about a dramatic improvement although the area of the bite is cold. In this picture, the patient won't let go of the ice pack!

Oxalicum acidum (**oxalic acid**). This remedy works well if the affected part becomes numb and cold to the touch and the victim also reports violent pains and begins to tremble. It's imperative to rush the victim to the nearest hospital! Give one dose of the remedy on your way.

Urtica urens (**stinging nettle**). This remedy is used for stings of jellyfish and medusa, as well as for any type of insect bites or stings in which the main symptoms are hives and itching that get better from rubbing the area. Some people in need of this remedy simply cannot stop rubbing the wound.

Burns

In December 2002 homeopaths Roger Morrison, M.D., and Nancy Herrick, P.A., happened to be in Bali during a terrorist bombing that caused massive damage and killed hundreds of people. Rushing to the local hospital to help, they discovered a scene of utter chaos.

Reporting in a *Homeopathy Today* article, Morrison explains that the majority of injuries were burns.

> *Nancy and I spent the first six hours debriding burns and changing dressings. Luckily we had a few homeopathic remedies with us—including* Arnica *and* Aconite 200C, *known for their effec-*

tiveness in cases of trauma and shock. It is a rare opportunity to see homeopathy working in cases so extreme, and the results in cases of shock were astonishing even to us. People who were lying paralyzed with fixed gaze began sitting up and speaking minutes after the remedy.[4]

Serious burns always have to be treated in a hospital setting. Burn victims may require intravenous fluids, pain medication, antibiotics, and other supplies. You shouldn't delay seeking professional medical attention in order to select the right remedy. Rush the burn victim to the hospital and give the best remedy you can en route there.

For minor burns, Hahnemann advised using warm applications, a practice that makes sense homeopathically. Of course, the majority of burn victims ask to be given cold applications. Folk medicine also recommends touching your own earlobe in cases of minor burns to the fingertips, as the earlobe is usually cold.

After cleaning the burned area and making sure it is dry, apply homeopathically prepared *Calendula* ointment or lotion. Then if the picture of the remedy's characteristic symptoms seems appropriate, give the burn victim one of the following remedies. Do not apply anything except for covering the area with dry sterile gauze if the burned area has blisters or boils. In this case, seek professional help immediately!

Note: if the victim is terrified by the traumatic experience of being burned, it is appropriate to give *Aconitum* instead of *Arnica*.

Apis mellifica (honeybee). This remedy is used for minor burns that are greatly relieved by ice-cold applications and that are red and swollen. This remedy is also helpful for treating chemical burns to the eyes.

Note: if you don't know how to handle chemical burns, don't interfere with the efforts of trained professionals or a first-response team.

Arsenicum album (arsenic trioxide). This remedy is beneficial for severe burns (third degree) and for burns accompanied by significant anxiety and restlessness. Note that the victim refuses cold applications and feels better from warm applications.

Cantharis (Spanish fly). This remedy is usually used for second-degree and third-degree burns with extreme burning pain. Unlike a patient in the *Arsenicum* state, this victim desires ice-cold applications. *Cantharis* works for chemical burns, too.

Note: a prompt administration of this remedy may prevent the formation of blisters.

Urtica urens (stinging nettle). This remedy is beneficial for minor burns caused by scalding hot boiling water.

FOCUS POINTS

Sudden onset ❀ High fever ❀ Confusion ❀ Sensitivity to light,
noise, and touch ❀ Red, hot, dry face with cold hands and/or feet
❀ No thirst during fever

 **6**

Belladonna

Your Homeopathic Pediatrician

*I have never been lost, but I will admit to being
confused for several weeks.*

— DANIEL BOONE

A GOOD PEDIATRICIAN IS always there for you and your child, within reach day and night to guide you through the many concerns of childhood, from sniffles and sneezes to more serious illnesses. Like an excellent pediatrician, *Belladonna (Atropa belladonna)* is extremely useful for handling a broad range of childhood disorders. It provides prompt relief for problematic conditions that include fever, colds and flu, earaches, sore throats, sunstroke, heat prostration, colic, and nightmares. Breast-feeding mothers also find it enormously helpful in relieving mastitis, or breast infection, which enables them to continue safely and comfortably nursing their infants.

When you think about *Belladonna*, remember the motto "A stitch in time saves nine." *Belladonna* states often occur in the early hours of an illness, at which time this extraordinary homeopathic remedy is capable of stopping even serious problems from progressing beyond initial fever and discomfort. A patient may only need a single dose.

How can you determine that someone needs this remedy and not a comparable one, such as *Aconitum*? People requiring *Belladonna* will always demonstrate a certain level of confusion, even sedation, along with enlarged pupils and a hot, red face. As you know after reading the last chapter, this state is distinct from the one that is improved by *Aconitum*. The following description of the remedy and the plant that it is derived from will help you clearly understand the signs that indicate a need for *Belladonna*.

The Origins of *Belladonna*

Belladonna grows in both Europe and Asia. Some naturalists suggest that it originated in India. In its crude form, the plant is known and used both for its medicinal properties and its hallucinogenic effects. Its Latin name, *Atropa belladonna*, is derived from two sources. *Atropa*, the genus appellation, comes from the ancient Greek word *atropos*, meaning "the inevitable." As the name of the eldest of the three Fates in Greek mythology, this is a reference to its poisonous nature. She was responsible for cutting the threads that are woven into the cloth of human life and dictating each person's ultimate destiny.

Belladonna means "beautiful lady" in both Spanish and Italian. Connecting this idea with the plant probably refers to a tradition in the medieval Spanish and Italian cultures for women to dilate their pupils by placing a drop of *Belladonna* in each eye. The application made their eyes glassy, and obviously this effect was perceived as highly attractive to the men living in that historical era. The juice of the plant was also used to cause the skin to appear paler, another desired feature of women in that period.

There is another, more dangerous, side of this plant's effects. Historians suggest that *Belladonna* juice would have been a part of sleeping potions concocted in the Elizabethan era, such as the fictitious one used by the lovers in Shakespeare's play *Romeo and Juliet*. *Belladonna* is a member of the Solanaceae, or nightshade, family, which includes such menacing relatives as the hairy henbane (*Hyosciamus niger*), whose raw essence is the foundation of a remedy effective in treating psychosis, and thornapple, the raw material for another useful homeopathic remedy, *Stramonium*.

Belladonna is striking in its appearance. In only a single season, its tall, hairy stem can reach a height of six feet. Leaves span up to ten inches in length. The plant flowers in July and August, producing large bell-shaped blossoms that later turn into large shiny black berries, which reach the size of cherries by September. Due to the combination of their poisonous nature and seductive sweet taste, the berries have been called devil's cherries and naughty man's cherries.

All parts of the plant are poisonous, even when taken in small quantities, and the sweet black berries are especially so. Some people have reported eating up to five of the berries and survived, but others have died from eating just one. Because the juice is so sweet it can, and has, attracted the taste buds of curious children, who then fall ill. Thus another name for *Belladonna* is deadly nightshade, a reference at least partially derived from the number of infant deaths associated with consuming the plant's berries.

The symptoms of poisoning from the natural deadly nightshade plant have been known for centuries. These include fever, dry mouth, rapid pulse, dilation of the pupils, headache, difficulty swallowing, hallucinations, nightmares, and convulsions, to name a few. Of course, as you understand well by now, these are exactly the kind of symptoms that homeopathically prepared *Belladonna* alleviates—like cures like. Based on the outcome from accidental poisonings and the results of numerous purposeful provings, we have fully cataloged the specific picture of the *Belladonna* state.

Like other poisonous plants, *Belladonna* is transformed into a parent's best friend as a result of the sophisticated process of serial dilutions and successions, which renders it harmless. Homeopathic preparations of *Belladonna* are completely safe—and potent. As a matter of fact, Dr. Hahnemann saved the lives of many children suffering from an epidemic of scarlet fever in 1801 using *Belladonna*. Perhaps more interestingly, he then discovered that *Belladonna* could be used to prevent future cases of the deadly illness. We'll talk more about that breakthrough discovery later, in the section on sore throats.

Symptoms Characteristic of the *Belladonna* State

Taking *Belladonna* can help any condition that begins with the following unique combination of symptoms:

* Sudden onset
* High fever
* Confusion
* Frequent sleepiness, yet cannot fall asleep
* Fear of imaginary objects
* Sensitivity to light, noise, and touch
* Eyes that are staring and glossy with enlarged pupils
* Red, hot, dry face with cold hands and/or feet
* No thirst during high fever, otherwise thirsty for lemonade or wants lemons
* Throbbing, bursting headache
* Any inflammation with a sensation of dryness, burning heat, and bright redness

Things that improve the condition:

* Standing or sitting up

Things that make the condition worse:

* Movement, even slight jarring
* Noise
* Light
* Lying down

Circumstances that may trigger this combination of symptoms include:

❀ Any acute infection, such as a cold or flu virus
❀ Exposure to sunlight and heat

Fever

The realities of life frequently offer amazing examples of how well homeopathy works.

One evening I was walking in downtown Manhattan with a colleague, a family physician, from the Continuum Center for Health and Healing, who was on call for pediatrics that night. Around 8 P.M. the doctor received a page asking him to phone a couple whose child had a high fever, and he suggested that I participate. He knew basic homeopathy and wanted to be sure he did the right thing if homeopathy could be employed.

During the phone conversation, the mother told my colleague that her six-year-old daughter had been seen for a cold earlier that same day by a pediatrician at the center. That pediatrician felt comfortable that the child didn't have a serious infection and suggested using homeopathy if a high fever developed. Now, according to the mother, the girl appeared red and hot and had a core temperature of 102. We asked her to touch her daughter's hands. They were cold. We asked about the girl's eyes. She told us that her daughter's pupils were large and her eyes looked glassy. The girl was slightly confused.

Based on the conversation, we had the following information: no serious infection was found earlier that day, the fever was high, and the girl showed the signs of needing *Belladonna*. Fortunately, the woman was prepared and had a few remedies on hand. We recommended that she give the child three pellets of *Belladonna* 30C and report back to us in an hour. That report was good. The child had gone to sleep soon after receiving the dose of pellets, and her fever was down. We made a suggestion to repeat the remedy using the plussing method (see Chapter 2) if the fever returned in the middle of the night. Our follow-up call the next day revealed no problems. The child was well.

Guess what? You could have done as good a job as we did and perhaps would face an even easier decision. After all, you have an advantage: you can see your little patient right in front of you. You also have the same safeguard if the problem continues: your pediatrician. Of course, it wouldn't hurt if your pediatrician read this book, too.

Belladonna is the homeopathic remedy most frequently needed to treat fever in children. Like *Aconitum*, it is most beneficial in the first few hours of fever. But its picture can be easily distinguished from the *Aconitum* picture. Someone who needs *Belladonna* has glassy eyes with enlarged pupils (compare with small pupils in the case of *Aconitum*). Those who need *Aconitum* are morbidly scared and extremely restless.

Symptoms are usually clear and include some degree of confusion, high fever, and feeling and looking hot and dry. Some patients may hallucinate and even become angry and bite. In some cases, you may notice slight twitching of the face and the body or even febrile seizures (caused by fever). There is no thirst at the height of the fever. But at other times, patients frequently ask for lemonade or lemons.

Let's briefly consider four other frequently indicated and easy-to-distinguish remedies. See Table 6.1 on pages 102–103 for a comparison chart.

Aconitum napellus (monkshood). Symptoms frequently begin after exposure to a chilling wind. In this state, the patient is excited, afraid, and restless. If this individual isn't excited and restless, *Aconitum* probably isn't a good choice of remedy.

Characteristic symptoms:

* Sudden onset
* Fear, especially fear of death (usually for no reason)
* Restlessness
* Small pupils
* Chill or extremely high fever
* Tremendous thirst

Bryonia alba (white bryony). This remedy is used for slowly progressing influenza and common colds in which muscular aching is one of the important symptoms. The key indication is the desire to be absolutely still, as the patient feels much worse from even the slightest movement. The patient does everything possible to save energy.
Characteristic symptoms:

* Feeling of internal restlessness but no tolerance for even the slightest movement
* Desire to be left alone, doesn't want to answer questions, irritability without expressing it aloud
* Fever with the pronounced sensation of heat
* Profuse perspiration
* Chills that begin distally (fingertips, toes, rarely the lips) and can be triggered by anger
* Great thirst for large gulps at intervals
* Severe headaches located on the front left side of the head or on the back of the head
* Worse symptoms generally on the right side of the body (except for the headache, which is on the left)
* Usually warm—worse in warm rooms
* Worse: frequently at 9 P.M. and from the slightest movement

Chamomilla (German chamomile). This remedy is especially useful for young children during teething and older kids (and adults) with intense, long-lasting fevers.
Characteristic symptoms:

* New teeth coming in
* Irritability and capriciousness
* Calms down only if carried in someone's arms
* One red cheek and the other pale (this rare symptom is only important in combination with other characteristic symptoms— use it as a final point of assessment)
* Very high fever with intolerable heat that does not come down for a long time

❀ Face and head that are hot and sweaty
❀ Thirst
❀ Worse: at 9 A.M. and/or at night, when the baby is angry, and from uncovering

Ferrum phosphoricum (phosphate of iron). The main feature of this remedy is that it has no specific symptoms. Unfortunately, this sometimes leads parents either not to use it at all or to use it every time their child has a fever. What's the real deal? A few hours after your child gets a fever, if you cannot find anything to report more specific than that the child is hot to touch and has a red face, odds are that he or she needs *Ferrum*.

Characteristic symptoms:

❀ Gradual onset of fever
❀ Headache that feels better from a cold compress
❀ Symptoms similar to those of the *Belladonna* state but with no confusion and milder
❀ Better: from cold applications, lying down (compare with the *Belladonna* state, which is the opposite), and touch (compare with the *Bryonia* state, in which the patient won't let you touch him)
❀ Worse: from movement and at night

Sunstroke and Heat Prostration

Frequently people think that sunstroke and heat prostration are the same condition. Actually, that's not true. Sunstroke develops suddenly and severely and includes a full, extremely rapid pulse. Heat prostration develops gradually, and its presentation is less dramatic, although equally dangerous. A child left sitting inside a car could easily get heat prostration, or a child at the beach on a bright day, sunstroke. When either condition occurs, the victim must be put in the shade and cooled off as quickly as possible.

Warning: if someone's skin is dry and very hot, or if the body temperature is rising quite rapidly, the situation can become life threatening. First aid is to pour cool water on the victim, apply ice, and give ice-cold drinks. Calling 911 is a must. Then while waiting for help to arrive, give the sufferer a homeopathic remedy.

Belladonna is indicated when there are high fever, burning dry and flushed skin, enlarged pupils, and a strong, rapid pulse. Frequently, *Belladonna* sunstroke develops after a person falls asleep in the sun. The sufferer might also exhibit confusion and all the other typical signs of *Belladonna*, including a pulsating headache. If someone in this condition becomes agitated (rare), *Belladonna* is almost a 100 percent correct choice.

Following are six of the most helpful alternative choices.

Aconitum napellus (**monkshood**). If you see symptoms of tremendous fear of death in combination with agitation (a rare occurrence in sunstroke victims), *Aconitum* would be your first choice.

❀ Sunstroke that comes on suddenly and with a violent intensity
❀ Constricted pupils

Carbo vegetabilis (**vegetable charcoal**).

❀ Fainting and collapse under any circumstances
❀ Feeling of being cold, clammy, and nauseous
❀ Better (much better): from fanning

Cuprum metallicum (**copper**).

❀ Severe cramps in abdomen and/or legs
❀ Pale face
❀ Extreme weakness (compare with *Veratrum*)

Gelsemium sempervirens (**yellow jasmine**).

❀ Headache in the back of the head (this is the most characteristic symptom)
❀ Severe weakness
❀ Feeling of trembling
❀ Vertigo and dizziness

Table 6.1 Fever Remedy Comparison Chart

Remedy	Onset	Better	Worse
Aconitum	Sudden	Open air	Exposure to cold air; warm room; evening and night, after midnight
Belladonna	Sudden	Lemonade; lemons	Afternoon, especially around 3 P.M.
Bryonia	Slow progression	Being alone (emotionally better)	Slightest movement; 9 P.M.
Chamomilla	Sudden	Being carried (emotionally better)	Dentition; being uncovered
Ferrum phosphoricum	Frequently sudden	Characteristically, no modalities	Characteristically, no modalities

Glonoine (**nitroglycerin**). This is the primary remedy for sunstroke.

❋ Violent pulsating headache with a feeling that the head will burst at any time
❋ Appearance that is similar to *Belladonna*, but with a headache significantly more violent
❋ Headache that feels better when wearing a hat

Emotional State	Signs Guiding Your Selection	Reasons to Say No to This Remedy
Fearful; anxious; restless; clinging to parents from fear	The very beginning of the illness; no discharges; small pupils; thirst for cold water; high fever and/or chills	Any discharge; late stages (more then a few hours) of illness; absence of fear or anxiety
Confused; may have hallucinations; may look sedated	Flushed face with cold hands and feet; dilated pupils; no thirst; frequently, right-sided pounding headache	Small pupils; low-grade fever; significant thirst; discharges; late stages (more than 24 hours) of illness
Wants to be left alone; refuses to answer questions; irritable	Tremendous thirst; fever with the sensation of heat and profuse perspiration; chills that begin from the fingertips and toes	Communicative; no thirst
Irritable; capricious	Teething in babies and older children; intolerable heat that does not come down; diarrhea	Mild tempered; gentle; constipated
Pleasant; good-natured	With the look of *Belladonna* but without characteristic modalities	Irritable; demanding; has unique modalities

* Hot, drowsy feeling
* Frequent urination

Veratrum album (white hellebore). This remedy is most useful in cases of heat exhaustion, which usually results from dehydration. The pulse is not as pounding as in sunstroke (it doesn't go higher than a hundred beats per minute), and:

❋ Skin that is cold and clammy
❋ Pale appearance and feelings of weakness and nausea

Earache

An earache usually signals the inflammation of the middle ear, or otitis media. Although this condition is often called acute otitis media, logically only the first episode could be considered acute. All subsequent cases in the same individual most probably indicate the development of a chronic condition. Prompt homeopathic treatment of the first episode usually halts the development of chronic earaches. If more than one earache does occur, it is imperative to see a trained homeopath to cure the chronic otitis. Untreated infections in the ears are potentially dangerous, as they can develop into meningitis, an inflammation of the membranes covering the brain and the spinal cord.

Pediatricians increasingly embrace the tactic of watchful waiting. If a child doesn't show obvious signs of severe infection, the pediatrician refrains from prescribing an antibiotic right away. This window of opportunity is a good time to try a homeopathic solution. You should also remember that the first symptoms, which only you get to see, could respond to homeopathy and quickly eliminate the ground for any future issues.

Belladonna is the main homeopathic remedy for sudden onset of a right-sided earache. In this state, the patient has a high fever, a flushed face, glassy eyes with enlarged pupils, and dry lips. Although the pain of the earache has a throbbing quality, very young children won't be able to appreciate or describe this distinction. So look closely at their behavior. Small children just grab onto or rub their right ear. Your child may be confused, have nightmares, and feel angry. In this state children often wake up screaming from fear and pain. Loud noises, touch, and light make the earache feel worse. It feels better when lying down (compare with *Chamomilla*).

Following are a few other important remedies for treatment of earaches. See Table 6.2 on pages 108–109 for a comparison chart.

Aconitum napellus (monkshood). This remedy is indicated for a sudden onset of severe pain after exposure to a cold wind or draft.

❊ Sudden onset
❊ Fear and restlessness (in a child)
❊ High fever
❊ Severe pain
❊ Flushed face
❊ Small pupils
❊ Significant thirst for cold drinks

Chamomilla (German chamomile). This remedy is often indicated for earaches that accompany teething. Characteristics are:

❊ Highly irritable, demanding, and capricious (for example, the child asks for something but refuses it the moment it is offered)
❊ Screams violently and calms down only if carried
❊ Desire not to be touched or even looked at
❊ Worse: from lying down

Ferrum phosphoricum (phosphate of iron). This is one of the most useful remedies at the beginning of an earache when you clearly see that there's a problem but it doesn't match any remedy you know. Although the picture of the condition is similar to the *Belladonna* state, it doesn't fit exactly—especially in the level of intensity. It just doesn't present the clear picture that someone who needs *Belladonna* usually does.

❊ Pain that is usually on the right side

Hepar sulphuris calcareum (calcium sulphide).

❊ Extreme sensitivity to the slightest interference (a cold draft, uncovering a part of a body, or a touch can make the pain seem a hundred times worse)
❊ Quickly flies into a rage (compare with *Chamomilla*: the child who needs *Chamomilla* calms down if constantly carried

around, and the *Hepar* child just doesn't want to be touched or bothered in any way—carrying such a child will only make things worse)

Pulsatilla nigricans (**windflower**). This is the most frequently required remedy in cases of earache that arises after the child has a cold with yellowish-greenish nasal discharge.

* ❀ Weepiness and need for affection
* ❀ Sweet and defenseless appearance
* ❀ Better: from fresh air and being gently carried (compare with the *Chamomilla* state, when a child would have been carried in a brisk, energetic way)
* ❀ Worse: from heat

Verbascum thapsus (**mullein**).

* ❀ Left-sided earache
* ❀ Hoarseness and possible deep-toned cough
* ❀ Better: after rising from a sitting position and from taking a deep breath
* ❀ Worse: from sitting, change of temperature, talking, biting teeth together, and in the evening

Sore Throat

Belladonna is an absolute leader in the treatment of acute sore throats. As I mentioned at the start of the chapter, Hahnemann became a veritable medical celebrity in 1801 due to his discovery of the tremendous value of *Belladonna* in treating scarlet fever, a severe form of strep throat. Only five years after homeopathy's official inception, an epidemic swept Germany. Children were the main victims. Through an experience in caring for children within the same family, some who got ill and some who did not, Hahnemann identified the curative power of *Belladonna* for most of the cases of scarlet fever occurring at that time.

Hahnemann achieved such impressive results in the treatment and prevention of deadly scarlet fever in 1801 that many allopathic physicians soon adopted his new approach and began praising homeopathy. The outcome was staggering. Ten physicians gave homeopathic *Belladonna* to 1,646 children for preventive care. They reported that only 123 patients developed the illness, whereas the morbidity rate in the untreated population surged as high as 90 percent! Subsequently, the top public health official in Germany declared the remedy effective. Other doctors were encouraged to adopt it.

Please don't rush out and start dosing your children willy-nilly with *Belladonna* this winter in hopes of avoiding strep throat, however. Later on Hahnemann and other homeopaths realized that the *Belladonna* success was merely a temporary solution. In many cases of strep throat, other remedies are required. It depends on the individual characteristics of the patient and the particular epidemiological situation in a particular area.

Bear in mind that homeopaths do not prescribe remedies for specific conditions, but rather for individual patients. It is only in rare cases of epidemics, when there are so many people at once suffering from an illness that a common remedy picture emerges. However, the remedy is specific only during that particular epidemic. *Belladonna* might be the right match for a community in New Jersey while another remedy might be right for a community in Kansas even if both are having outbreaks of the same disease.

Typical symptoms that call for the use of *Belladonna* for the treatment of a sore throat include:

❀ Pain and burning on the right side
❀ No tolerance for even a slight touch of the throat
❀ High fever with a red face
❀ Large pupils
❀ Hot, red head, and cold hands and feet
❀ Possible confusion (in children)

Table 6.2 Earache Remedy Comparison Chart

Remedy	Onset	Better	Worse
Aconitum	Sudden	No specific modalities	No specific modalities
Belladonna	Sudden	Warm applications	Jarring; after midnight
Chamomilla	Sudden	Being constantly carried and rocked	Touch (doctors, beware of even trying to examine this child!)
Ferrum phosphoricum	Sudden	Cold applications	Night
Hepar sulphuris	Sudden	Ear and the rest of the the body being wrapped to protect from the slightest motion of the air; warmth	Movement of cold air around the ear; night
Pulsatilla	Gradual	Open or cool air; being gently held and gently carried	Heat; night
Verbascum	Nonspecific	No specific modalities	Biting hard; talking; sneezing

Emotional State	Signs Guiding Your Selection	Reasons to Say No to This Remedy
Scared; restless	Symptoms appear more often on left side; sudden onset with severe pain, high fever, flushed face, small pupils; afraid; significant thirst for cold drinks	Gradual onset; enlarged pupils
Confused (could even be hallucinating)	Symptoms appear more often on right side; high fever; severe pulsating pain; often, red ear; red, hot face with cold extremities; glassy eyes with large pupils; no thirst	Thirst; small pupils
Very angry and demanding (this little tyrant torments the family)	Extreme sensitivity to pain; violent screaming from pain; irritability; demandingness; capriciousness	Mild-mannered child
Usually sweet disposition but no specific symptoms	Symptoms appear most often on right side; sudden onset with high fever; may appear to need *Belladonna* but no modalities	Clear modalities indicating other remedies
Irritable; extremely sensitive to pain (screams from pain)	Extreme sensitivity to even the slightest motion of the air and to cold; pain made better by nothing except for being covered; desire to have the ear bundled up; sensation of a splinter stuck in the ear	Desire to be uncovered; better from being carried
Mild mannered; weepy; wants affection and consolation	More common in left ear; ear infection that begins with cold and greenish discharge from the nose; weepiness; mild mannered; need for attention	Anger; desire not to be touched; likes heat
No specific picture	Severe left-sided earache; hoarse voice; deep-toned cough	Right-sided complaints

Following are seven other helpful remedies.

Aconitum napellus (monkshood).

❉ Sudden beginning of a sore throat after exposure to cold, windy weather
❉ Very severe symptoms
❉ Fear and restlessness
❉ Thirst for cold drinks that are painful to swallow (compare with *Phytolacca decandra*)

Ferrum phosphoricum (phosphate of iron). The most specific symptom of this remedy is a lack of specific symptoms. Use for the following:

❉ Sore throat with high to moderate fever
❉ Gradual onset of the illness
❉ Significant weakness

Hepar sulphuris calcareum (calcium sulphide).

❉ Extreme irritability at the slightest provocation
❉ Extreme sensitivity to pain and suffering
❉ Chill with a cold sweat
❉ Splinterlike pains (almost like a fish bone) in the throat (make sure the pain isn't actually from a fish bone, because if it is, the remedy isn't what is needed—rather, the bone has to be removed)
❉ No difficulty swallowing liquids but pain on swallowing solids (compare with *Lachesis muta*)

Lachesis muta (bushmaster snake venom). This is a great remedy that was discovered by Dr. Hering.

❉ Exclusively left-sided symptoms
❉ Extreme sensitivity in the neck—no tolerance even for a slight pressure from tight collars

❀ Better: from cold drinks and temporary relief from swallowing solid food (compare with *Hepar sulphuris*)

❀ Worse: from swallowing saliva and hot drinks, on waking up, and with heat

Mercurius vivus (quicksilver).

❀ Frequently (but not always) indicated for right-sided sore throats

❀ Slow onset

❀ Offensive breath

❀ Increased salivation, especially at night

❀ Increased perspiration

❀ Dirty-looking, thick, coated tongue with teeth imprints on the edges

❀ Metallic taste

❀ Neck glands that are frequently swollen and tender

❀ Worse (much worse): at night and with empty swallowing

Mercurius iodatus ruber (biniodide of mercury).

❀ Frequently indicated for left-sided sore throat

❀ All other symptoms similar to *Mercurius vivus*, from which this remedy is derived

Phytolacca decandra (poke root).

❀ Raw, swollen, and burning throat

❀ Painful swallowing that radiates into ears

❀ Feeling of a hot lump

❀ Pain at the root of the tongue and/or on the palate right above the tongue

❀ Tongue coated and with a red tip

❀ Neck glands frequently enlarged and painful (similar to both of the *Mercurius* remedies)

❀ Better: from cold drinks

❀ Worse: from hot drinks

Table 6.3 Sore Throat Remedy Comparison Chart

Remedy	Onset	Better	Worse
Aconitum	Sudden	No specific modalities	Cold drinks that are highly desired but painful to swallow
Belladonna (main remedy for acute sore throat)	Sudden	No specific modalities	Touch to the throat; any motion that involves the throat area; swallowing liquids
Ferrum phosphoricum	Sudden	No specific modalities	Night
Hepar sulphuris	Sudden	Warm drinks; warm wraps of the throat	Cold drinks; movement of cold air around throat; night
Lachesis	At night or on waking up	Cold drinks; very brief relief from swallowing	Waking up; touching the throat; tight collars; night (may wake up in the middle of the night from being sick)
Mercurius vivus (often for right-sided pain)	No specific timing	No specific modalities	Swallowing; heat; warmth of bed; extreme warmth or cold; night
Mercurius iodatus ruber (exclusively for left-sided pain)	No specific timing	No specific modalities	Same as *Mercurius vivus*
Phytolacca (often for right-sided pain)	No specific timing	Cold drinks	Hot drinks

Emotional State	Signs Guiding Your Selection	Reasons to Say No to This Remedy
Scared; restless	Sudden onset; high fever; flushed face; small pupils; feeling of terror; significant thirst for cold drinks	Gradual onset; enlarged pupils
Confused, could even be hallucinating	Sudden onset of right-sided complaints; red, hot face with cold extremities; large pupils; no thirst	Thirst; small pupils
Usually has sweet disposition; no specific symptoms	Significant weakness; prostration	Clear modalities indicating other remedies
Irritable	Extreme sensitivity to even the slightest motion of the air and cold; desire to stay bundled up with the throat covered; sensation of a splinter stuck in the throat	Desire to be uncovered; better from cold drinks (think about *Phytolacca* or *Lachesis*)
Intense; can be very talkative (can't stop talking despite the pain)	Exclusively for left-sided pain or when the problem starts on the left and goes to the right; sensation of constriction of a lump in the throat; possibly, purple-colored tonsils	Relaxed feeling; right-sided complaints; no feeling of constriction
No specific modalities related to acute illness	Offensive breath; intense drooling, especially at night; swollen, painful glands on the neck; metallic taste; coated, dirty-looking tongue with tooth imprints; significant perspiration	Lack of specific symptoms
No specific modalities	Similar to *Mercurius vivus*	Right-sided tonsillitis without typical mercurial symptoms
No specific modalities	Burning, raw throat; enlarged glands on the neck	Can drink hot liquids; no feeling of burning in the throat

A Few More Conditions That May Require *Belladonna*

An amazingly large number of babies with colic require the administration of *Belladonna*. The key symptom to look for is that these children get better from lying on the belly. You can read more about this ailment in Chapter 7.

Another serious problem that a large number of children in the modern world face is nightmares. Although not described in great detail in this book, this problem frequently responds to a single dose of *Belladonna*, provided the child presents with other characteristic symptoms of this remedy. Bear in mind, however, that another important remedy to consider for nightmares is *Stramonium*. The combination of terrible nightmares, night terrors, fear of the dark, and fear of dogs almost certainly indicates a need for *Stramonium*.

Belladonna can be helpful with a large number of acute and chronic ailments ranging from seizure disorders to ovarian cysts and sinusitis, but finding a correct remedy for these conditions should be left up to a professional homeopath.

FOCUS POINTS

Extreme irritability ❀ High sensitivity to even the slightest pain ❀ Desire not
to be touched or spoken to ❀ Capriciousness ❀ Ailments during teething
❀ Improved by being constantly carried

 **7**

Chamomilla
Your Homeopathic Babysitter

*I am sorry to say that Peter was not very well during
the evening. His mother put him to bed, and made
some chamomile tea; and she gave a dose of it to Peter!
"One tablespoon to be taken at bedtime."*

—BEATRIX POTTER, *THE TALE OF PETER RABBIT*

CHAMOMILLA (*Matricaria recutita*, German chamomile) has been
known for centuries for its calming effect on children. That's why
we're calling it a homeopathic babysitter—and it's a good one, too.
Chamomilla can help your child get through colic and problems with
teething. It relieves pain, subdues anger, and eases the fear of a child
frightened of dentists and surgeons. The children (and sometimes
the adults) who need *Chamomilla* always act enormously irritable,
angry, demanding, and capricious.

You can easily recognize a child who needs *Chamomilla* just from
hearing shocking screams in the background while you're having a

115

phone conversation with a friend who has a baby or a toddler. In adults a good example of the *Chamomilla* state would be the pregnant woman who screams her lungs out during childbirth, cursing at her husband and everyone else in the delivery room for "all the pain they've caused." A woman in this state asks for something she "really needs" and then rejects it the moment it's brought to her. She's impulsive, unpredictable, and inconsistent.

The Origins of *Chamomilla*

Native to Europe and Asia, German chamomile has been grown successfully in Australia and North America. Some gardeners call it true chamomile, as it is frequently confused with so-called Roman chamomile, a plant many people use for making lawns because the more you run on it, the faster it grows. But German chamomile and Roman chamomile actually belong to different species. Egyptians worshiped chamomile for its medicinal properties, which were rediscovered by Europeans in the Middle Ages when it was applied to children's ailments, nausea, nervous complaints, and skin diseases. In that period, it was also considered to be helpful for diseases of the kidneys and spleen, bladder troubles, colds, and malaria, as well as to expel worms. Chamomile tea was believed to make an excellent wash for sore and weak eyes. It was also used as a poultice for pain and swellings.[1]

In *The New Honest Herbal*, Varro E. Tyler writes about herbal chamomile: "As a popular remedy, it may be thought of as the European counterpart of ginseng."[2] He also mentions that the Germans call the plant *alles zutraut*, "capable of anything." Traditionally, chamomile root was chewed to reduce toothache.

Gardeners who practice the biodynamic method of growing plants use German chamomile as an important fertilizer. Drooping and dying plants have been observed to recover if German chamomile is planted near them. It also stimulates the growth of grain. Old herbal books called chamomile the plant physician.

Unlike *Aconitum* and *Belladonna*, the German chamomile plant does not have an impressive, dangerous, or distinguished look.

Rather, it looks like the kind of wildflower whose petals a lover plucks when pining, "She loves me, she loves me not." It is a strange contradiction that a beautiful plant would be so useful for patients who are a disaster. We expect pregnant women or an innocent child to be angelic, and our expectations are defied when they behave like devils. Heaven meets hell. Considering the long history of the allopathic use of this herb to soothe severe complaints and its innocent look, you would probably not expect it to cause severe symptoms, exactly the opposite of its appearance.

Symptoms Characteristic of the *Chamomilla* State

Eminent American homeopath Margaret Tyler wrote this about *Chamomilla*: "An excellent name for *Chamomilla* is 'cannot bear it'— Can't bear himself. Can't bear other people. Can't bear pain. Can't bear things; wants them, and hurls them away. Everything is simply intolerable." She also states, "Despite this picture of gentility, this is the remedy that cannot return a civil answer."[3]

N. M. Choudhuri, a prominent Indian homeopath, called *Chamomilla* the "ugliest remedy."[4] The children—and sometimes the adults—who need homeopathic *Chamomilla* bring misery wherever they go. They have the worst temper tantrums you can possibly imagine. They scream and cry, kick and bite, throw themselves on the floor and bend backward, practically driving their parents and everyone around them to despair.

Chamomilla can help any condition that begins with the following unique combination of symptoms:

* ❀ Loud, constant screaming
* ❀ Extreme irritability
* ❀ Angry, whining, demanding behavior
* ❀ High sensitivity to even the slightest pain (may perspire from even the slightest pain or may even faint from pain)
* ❀ Desire not to be touched or spoken to

❀ Capriciousness (asks for things that are immediately rejected when delivered)
❀ Better: from being constantly carried; toothache better from cold
❀ Worse: from sun, open air, night, and heat

You may have heard or read about an unusual characteristic of the *Chamomilla* state: one cheek is hot and red, while the other cheek is cold and pale. Although this symptom is described in every single book I've read on homeopathy, people rarely develop it. I have never seen this symptom in my twenty-plus years of private practice. Some people do develop it, just not often. Of course, if you ever do see this particular indicator in combination with other important traits of the *Chamomilla* state, you can use it to confirm your choice. However, if you see all the other symptoms except for this one, please go ahead and give the remedy. You likely still have a match.

Circumstances that involve this combination of symptoms may include:

❀ Teething
❀ Earache
❀ Colic
❀ Childbirth (when a woman is screaming and yelling from severe, intolerable pain, look for other key symptoms of *Chamomilla*)
❀ Diarrhea (also see Chapter 10, pages 184–192)

Screaming Babies

We all know too well how disturbing a screaming baby can be. Babies cannot tell us what is wrong. We know they are suffering, but it is hard to understand the reason. My wife and I had a baby like this, and, I'll tell you, we had to come up with various sophisticated ways to calm her down. If you have a screaming baby, please ensure that there's nothing seriously wrong going on. A visit to a pediatrician is an excellent idea, as a first step.

The overwhelming majority of screaming babies come out of the pediatrician's office the same way they went in: screaming and with parents and a doctor who have no clue about what's going on. But they do have an important piece of information. There is nothing terribly wrong or else the pediatrician would have detected it. They also know the baby is in pain. But they don't know why. In newborns extended screaming is called colic. In older infants this behavior is usually due to teething. Both conditions may be accompanied by diarrhea or constipation.

Homeopathy can do miracles for screaming babies. The key to selecting a remedy in such cases is to try to understand what makes the baby feel better or feel worse. If you have tried your best without a result, it is a good time to visit a professional homeopath.

A screaming baby in a *Chamomilla* state shows characteristics typical of the remedy. Most of the babies are healthy and react to the reason that causes pain in a distinct manner. I will always remember the screams of a baby who needs *Chamomilla*. The sound is loud and demanding. It can only be stopped by holding or rocking the baby and walking around. The moment you put the baby down, the screaming begins again.

Frequently, babies in this state indicate—and toddlers tell you—that they want something but immediately reject it if offered. You simply cannot please this group. They are sensitive to noise and odors. They start to nurse and then become irritable and pull off. They may bite the nipple or strike you if they are older. Teething and colic in combination with green, spinachlike diarrhea, or teething with an earache are common signs that your baby or toddler would benefit from taking *Chamomilla*.

When dosing an infant, remember to try one of the two methods described in Chapter 2 (see page 23), where the remedy is diluted in water.

One dose of *Chamomilla* 30C is usually sufficient to soothe a screaming infant. If you see an improvement and then the baby complains (screams) again in a few hours or the next day, repeat the dose. With the correct remedy, the need for repetition will become less and less frequent. Often one dose of the remedy takes care of the entire problem.

Now let's talk about other options for screaming babies who do not present with a typical *Chamomilla* picture.

Colic

Amy Rothenberg, N.D., a respected homeopath and naturopathic physician who treats a lot of children, frequently asks the mothers of colicky babies to drink some nonalcoholic beer a half hour or so before nursing.[5] In her experience this helps the mother to relax due, most probably, to the ingredient hops. I suggest drinking hops tea instead of beer. The main objective here is to break the cycle of a nervous mother, which leads to a crying baby, which in turn leads to a nervous mother and crying baby, and so on.

Sometimes a baby will do better if the nursing mother avoids vegetables in the Brassicaceae family, including horseradish, radish, bok choy (Chinese mustard), pe tsai (Chinese cabbage), spinach mustard, turnip, broccoli, kale, cauliflower, cabbage, brussels sprouts, kohlrabi, and watercress. Although not members of the same family, onions and garlic are not recommended either. If the baby is on a formula, changing it can also help.

Many of you already know about and practice such precautions— remove certain foods from the diet, change the baby formula, and so on—but your baby still has colic! What can you do? Now is the time to turn to homeopathy.

As you proceed, remember that seeing the lack of a complete improvement after homeopathy is not necessarily the result of giving your child the wrong remedy, although that is possible. Instead, it could be due to a birth trauma to the head and spine or dietary intolerances, such as allergies to milk, soy, or something in the mom's diet.

We already discussed necessary dietary adjustments for mother and child. If you suspect birth trauma, a visit to a good osteopath who does craniosacral therapy may also bring about a dramatic improvement.

Following are eleven homeopathic remedies that could apply if *Chamomilla* is not the answer.

Aethusa cynapium (fool's parsley). This is often the right remedy for babies who are unable to tolerate milk or mother's milk.

❊ Vomiting of milk in curds soon after nursing

❊ Colicky and irritable behavior after vomiting (child may then go to sleep)

❊ Hunger after vomiting

❊ Vomiting possibly accompanied by greenish diarrhea

❊ Worse: in the evening and from 3 to 4 A.M., as well as from exertion and hot weather

Belladonna (deadly nightshade). If necessary, review Chapter 6.

❊ Distended, hot abdomen with protruding lumps

❊ Hot, red, dry face

❊ Dilated pupils

❊ Sensitivity to jarring, light, and noise (compare with a person in the *Chamomilla* state, who wants to be rocked)

❊ Possible high fever

❊ Violent pains that come in waves, appearing and disappearing suddenly

❊ Better: from bending backward, dark room, rest, and lying on the abdomen

❊ Worse: from touch and pressure

Bryonia alba (white bryony). This presentation may remind you a lot of *Chamomilla*. The main differences are that with *Bryonia alba*, symptoms include:

❊ Slightest motion (even coughing) creates severe pain

❊ Wants to be left alone (compare with *Chamomilla* and *Pulsatilla nigricans*)

❊ Very thirsty (compare with *Pulsatilla nigricans*)

Cina (wormseed). This may remind you of *Chamomilla* in its presentation. The main differences are that with *Cina*, symptoms include:

❊ Hard abdomen

❊ Dissatisfied, angry, does not want to be looked at

❊ Always hungry but develops diarrhea or vomiting after food

* Grinding of teeth or gums
* Itching anus and/or nose
* Better: from lying on the abdomen, motion, and being carried (compare with *Chamomilla*)
* Worse: from touch, much worse at night (the babies are frequently OK all day but scream their lungs out at night)

Colocynthis (bitter cucumber).

* Writhing in pain, pulling legs up to the abdomen
* Extreme irritability, restlessness, but still not calm if carried (compare with *Chamomilla* and *Pulsatilla nigricans*)
* Colic after anger
* Better: from hard pressure (parents hoist the baby up and over the shoulder to provide hard pressure) and bending forward
* Worse: at night and from lying on the abdomen

Ignatia amara (St. Ignatius's bean). This remedy is for a colicky baby whose mother has endured a significant loss (for example, a divorce or the death of her husband, her mother, another close relative, or a friend) during pregnancy or breast-feeding. Another common stressful situation is immigration or a relocation during which personal connections are severed and the mother grieves the loss of friends. A dose of *Ignatia amara* 30C for the baby and 200C for the mother may relieve the baby's colic and ease the mother's emotional pain.

Lycopodium (club moss).

* Anxious look, with a wrinkled brow and a worried expression
* Bloated
* Better: from passing gas or burping and from warm bottle held to the belly
* Worse: from 4 to 8 P.M., at 2 A.M., or sometimes all night

Magnesium phosphoricum (phosphate of magnesia). A baby with colic in this state is helped if the baby's knees can be kept up near the chest, as this seems to relieve bloating and gas. The baby will also settle down some if he or she can manage to let out a good burp.

❋ Better: from warmth, warm drinks, and gentle pressure on the abdomen (compare with *Colocynthis*, which is better from firm pressure and doubling up)

Nux vomica (Quaker buttons).

❋ Constipated (has to push hard with each bowel movement)
❋ Anger and irritability (carrying around or comforting does not help)
❋ Stuffy nose
❋ Better: from being very warm and drinking warm drinks
❋ Worse: from cold and eating and in the morning

Pulsatilla nigricans (windflower).

❋ Hiccoughs soon after eating
❋ Rumbling in the belly
❋ Gentle behavior, possible tearfulness, but no screaming or demanding
❋ No thirst (but likes to nurse for a long time for comfort)
❋ Better: (much better) from gentle rocking (compare with *Chamomilla* state, which requires constant rocking)

Rheum officinale (rhubarb).

❋ Changeable desires (similar to *Chamomilla*), but instead of being capricious and rejecting everything offered, the child dislikes just his or her favorite thing or wants just one particular thing
❋ Sour smell to the body and all discharges (for example, diarrhea)
❋ Better: from bending double and warmth
❋ Worse: from uncovering any part and eating

Table 7.1 Colic Remedy Comparison Chart

Remedy	Onset	Better	Worse
Aethusa	Soon after feeding	Company; open air	Heat; summer; evening
Belladonna	Comes and goes suddenly	Lying on the belly; bending (forward or backward)	Jarring
Bryonia	No particular pattern	Lying still	Slightest motion (even a parent trying to sit on the bed)
Chamomilla (the most common remedy)	Sudden	Being constantly carried and rocked; warm applications	Being left alone; night
Cina	Sudden	Lying on the belly; being carried over the shoulder; daytime	Night
Colocynthis (a common remedy)	Sudden	Hard pressure; bending forward; thrashing about; heat	Night
Ignatia	No specific timing	Eating (paradoxical modality)	Warm applications; morning
Lycopodium	4 to 8 P.M.	Warm applications; warm drinks; passing gas and/or burping (which provide temporary relief)	Eating

Emotional State	Signs Guiding Your Selection	Remedy to Compare With
Irritable; crying	Vomits curds of milk soon after nursing; gets colicky, irritable, exhausted, and then goes to sleep	*Pulsatilla*
Confused (could even be hallucinating)	Pains that appear and disappear suddenly; improvement from lying on the belly; distended abdomen with protruding lumps	*Cina*
Irritable; wants to be left alone	Much worse from even the slightest motion; thirst for cold drinks	*Chamomilla*
Restless; very angry and demanding (this little tyrant torments the family)	Extreme sensitivity to pain; angry crying with arching of the back; desire to be constantly carried and rocked	*Cina; Colocynthis; Rheum*
Angry; does not want to be looked at	OK all day, and then screams lungs out all night; always hungry	*Belladonna; Chamomilla; Rheum; Jalapa* (a rare remedy characterized by baby who seems to sleep all day and cry all night)
Irritable; extremely restless from pain	Severe pain (pulls legs up to the abdomen and thrashes about in pain); not better from being carried; better from hard pressure	*Belladonna; Chamomilla; Cina; Magnesium*
Changeable emotional state	Babies of mothers who are under significant emotional stress or in a family where there is a lot of stress (arguments, divorce, death)	*Chamomilla*
Looks anxious with wrinkled brow	Abdominal distention with gurgling and gas; much worse from 4 to 8 P.M.	*Pulsatilla*

continued

Table 7.1 Colic Remedy Comparison Chart (continued)

Remedy	Onset	Better	Worse
Nux vomica	Morning	Bowel movement; warm applications	Before passing a stool
Magnesium phosphoricum (a common remedy)	Sudden	Warm, even hot, applications; bending double; hard pressure	Cold; touch; night
Pulsatilla	Gradual	Being gently held and gently carried; nursing	Heat; night
Rheum	Sudden	Bending double; warmth	Uncovering; eating; moving

Teething

Some babies have absolutely no problems teething, but the majority of babies do have problems. For that group, homeopathic *Chamomilla* is the hands-down champion. Some experts believe that it is indicated in about 50 percent of cases. Nonetheless, it helps only those babies who present a typical *Chamomilla* picture. Don't forget the telltale signs of *Chamomilla* children: green, spinachlike diarrhea, and/or an earache that coincides with teething.

Let's look at other helpful remedies for painful and also difficult, slow teething. Remedies for slow teething should be given only once, at a dose of three pellets of 30C. See Table 7.2 starting on page 130 for a comparison chart of the remedies.

Aconitum napellus (monkshood).

❋ Painful teething
❋ High fever

Emotional State	Signs Guiding Your Selection	Remedy to Compare With
Irritable; very sensitive to all external stimuli impressions	Colic before stool or when attempting to pass a stool	*Chamomilla; Colocynthis; Rheum*
Significantly milder than those who need *Colocynthis*	Much improvement from warm applications on the abdomen	*Colocynthis*
Gentle; tearful; seeks comfort from mother	Mild mannered; much improvement from being carried gently and from nursing	*Chamomilla*
Dislikes one usually favorite thing or just asks for one particular thing	Sour smell of the body and all discharges	*Chamomilla; Colocynthis; Magnesium*

* Perspiration and thirst (compare with *Belladonna*)
* Small pupils
* Hot, red cheeks and cold extremities
* Tossing and turning during sleep (in the case of children)
* Biting their fists and screaming (in the case of babies)

Belladonna (deadly nightshade).

* Painful teething
* High fever
* No perspiration and no thirst (compare with *Aconitum*)
* Large pupils
* Hot, red cheeks and cold extremities
* Anger about the pains (child may even bite self or other people)

Calcarea carbonica (calcium carbonate).

❋ Slow, difficult teething
❋ Frequent colds and coughs
❋ Easygoing but stubborn behavior
❋ Usually large or plump (in the case of children)
❋ Love of eggs and milk
❋ Perspiration on the head

Calcarea phosphorica (calcium phosphate).

❋ Slow, difficult teething
❋ Rapid tooth decay
❋ Delayed closure of fontanels on top of the head
❋ Discontent and peevishness (child has a tendency to whine and moan; although not correct from the purist point of view, you could call this remedy chronic *Chamomilla*, as it works for more systemic, chronic cases)
❋ Child is usually skinny
❋ Loves smoked meats, ham, and bacon

Kreosotum (beechwood creosote). Although the picture of *Kreosotum* may remind you of the *Chamomilla* state, the main differences are:

❋ Very difficult, painful teething accompanied by coughing
❋ Constant, dry cough
❋ Fever without perspiration
❋ Severe caries (teeth often decay almost immediately after they come in)
❋ Cross, willful, obstinate behavior (child is easily vexed over trifles)

Phytolacca decandra (poke root). This is a remedy for acute teething problems. Its main indication is an irresistible urge to bite the teeth (or gums) together and sometimes also to bite people, but without typical *Belladonna* symptoms. The motivation is just to bite, not to hurt anyone.

Rheum officinale (rhubarb). Although the picture is similar to *Chamomilla*, major distinctions include:

❖ Painful teething with colic and sour pasty diarrhea
❖ Sour smell to the body and all discharges
❖ Sour mood

Silica (silicon dioxide).

❖ Slow, difficult teething
❖ Frequent colds and coughs (compare with *Calcarea carbonica*)
❖ Child is bright, but shy and stubborn
❖ Perspiring head and neck
❖ Feet that frequently perspire profusely and give off an unpleasant smell
❖ Clammy hands
❖ Chill

A Few More Conditions That May Require *Chamomilla*

While most people, using conventional logic, might presume that the best homeopathic remedy to reverse the negative effects of caffeine, such as the jitters and insomnia, would be the preparation *Coffea cruda*, in reality *Chamomilla* is the best antidote. This proves that homeopathy employs the principle of "similars," not the principle of "the same."

I don't know about you, but I am afraid of dentists. They drill, you know, and that can be painful. As a child I couldn't tolerate dental pain and drilling at all. Unfortunately, my parents and doctors knew nothing about homeopathy. Well, you and I know what to do, don't we? Here is an interesting case that was aided by *Chamomilla*.

Table 7.2 Teething Remedy Comparison Chart

Remedy	Urgent Help or Chronic Treatment Needed	Better	Worse
Aconitum	Urgent	No specific modalities	No specific modalities
Belladonna	Urgent	No specific modalities	Jarring; late evening and night
Calcarea carbonica	Chronic	Warm applications (but worse from warm food)	Warm food
Calcarea phosphorica	Chronic	Warm application	Damp, cold weather
Chamomilla (the most common remedy)	Urgent	Being constantly carried and rocked; cold drinks	At night in bed; cold air; warm food and drinks; night
Kreosotum (this remedy is difficult to distinguish from *Chamomilla*; when in doubt, start with *Chamomilla*)	Urgent	Warm applications; motion	Cold; rest
Phytolacca	Urgent	Biting something	No specific modalities for this condition

Emotional State	Signs Guiding Your Selection	Remedy to Compare With
Screams; bites own fists	High fever; small pupils; perspiration and thirst; interestingly, tooth pain in nursing mothers	*Belladonna; Chamomilla*
Angry when in pain; might try to bite other people	High fever; large pupils; no perspiration; no thirst	*Aconitum; Chamomilla; Phytolacca*
Easygoing but very stubborn	Slow, painful dentition in a large child who is easygoing and loves eggs and milk; perspiration on the head; stubbornness	*Calcarea phosphorica; Silica*
Discontented and peevish	Slow, painful dentition in a skinny, whining, moaning child who loves smoked meats, ham, and bacon; perspiration on the head	*Calcarea carbonica; Chamomilla* (many call *Calcarea phosphorica* remedy chronic *Chamomilla*); *Silica*
Irritable; screaming; wants to be carried all the time; capricious	Extreme sensitivity to pain; angry crying with arching of the back; need to be constantly carried and rocked; dentition that is frequently accompanied by colic with green diarrhea	*Belladonna; Calcarea phosphorica*
Cross; willful; asks for many things, but throws them all away (capricious)	Painful dentition accompanied by coughing; teeth that decay very quickly	*Chamomilla*
No specific modalities for this condition	Need to bite something (frequently winds up biting own teeth or gums or other people (but not from anger like *Belladonna*)	*Belladonna*

continued

Table 7.2 Teething Remedy Comparison Chart *(continued)*

Remedy	Urgent Help or Chronic Treatment Needed	Better	Worse
Rheum	Urgent	Being constantly carried	At night in bed
Silica	Chronic	Warm applications	Warm drinks; biting

Four-year-old Alex had been a patient of mine for a while. In that time, he'd made tremendous progress from being a sickly boy with serious sinusitis and asthma to being a much stronger young gentleman. At the time of this episode, my communication with his mother was mostly on the phone about twice a year. Whenever Alex got a cold of some kind, she'd call to ask what to do. Acute homeopathic prescribing always did the trick.

On this occasion, Alex was scheduled to see a dentist the next morning but had suddenly developed a severe earache. His mom called my cell phone at 10 P.M. for help. Fortunately for her and Alex, but unfortunately for my ears, I easily picked up a terrible sound. Alex was screaming like a whale! If I hadn't known this woman and the principles of homeopathy, I might have called 911 to report an attempted murder. I suggested that Alex's mother move away from the little screamer so I could hear the full story.

Well, Alex was in pain. He was rubbing his ear, had a high fever, and was experiencing diarrhea that looked like a green kind of unformed stool. You guessed it already, I'm sure. These are characteristics of *Chamomilla*. I decided to make certain and asked what was making Alex feel better. His mom told me that giving him his favorite toys was useless, he threw them away one by one as they

CHAMOMILLA: Your Homeopathic Babysitter

Emotional State	Signs Guiding Your Selection	Remedy to Compare With
Irritable, "sour" mood; specifically dislikes things that were once preferred or specifically asks for a particular thing	Sour smell of the body and all discharges; combination of teething with colic and sour pasty diarrhea	*Chamomilla*
Irritable and stubborn; can be very shy	Frequent infections; disproportionally large head in a skinny, sickly child; offensive perspiration, especially of feet	*Calcarea carbonica; Calcarea phosphorica*

arrived. The only thing that worked was constantly carrying him around or rocking him. That clinched it.

I prescribed a dose of *Chamomilla* 30C for Alex to be repeated in fifteen minutes if his improvement was less than 50 percent. It worked. Alex got better quickly, and we were all able to go to sleep afterward. The next morning, Alex's mom gave him one more dose of *Chamomilla*. It worked beautifully. They went to see the dentist and the boy behaved like an angel. The dentist was impressed.

Listen—I don't want anybody else to call me at night with a baby screaming bloody murder in the background. Please learn about *Chamomilla*! OK?

With the advances of modern dentistry, toothaches are becoming much more rare. Nonetheless, they occasionally occur. Those who get toothaches know how painful and impossible they are to tolerate. *Chamomilla* can help a person who is extremely sensitive to pain. For such people, one or two doses of three pellets of *Chamomilla* 30C can make a tremendous difference, both to help contain the pain and to help tolerate the drilling that is inevitably going to follow. Visits to a dentist would become so much easier if those who can't tolerate pain of any kind took it an hour before and again immediately prior to the visit.

FOCUS POINTS

Gradual onset ❁ Significant weakness, possibly trembling ❁ Heaviness in the head, especially in the back ❁ Heavy eyelids and limbs ❁ Anticipation anxiety

 **8**

Gelsemium
Your Homeopathic Neurologist

Some days it is a heroic act just to refuse the paralysis of fear and straighten up and step into another day.

—EDWARD ALBERT

GELSEMIUM SEMPERVIRENS (yellow jasmine, false jasmine, Carolina jessamine) is one of the most useful homeopathic remedies we have for treating neurological disorders and acute anxiety. As you may recall from Chapter 4, it is also frequently used to treat the flu. All parts of the plant from which the remedy is made are poisonous and cause gradual paralysis, which is the reason that it is required in cases where symptoms develop gradually and why it is important in treating problems affecting the brain, spine, and nerves, including conditions such as motor paralysis of the eyes, throat, or limbs, multiple sclerosis, myasthenia gravis, and Parkinson's disease.

In cases that require *Gelsemium*, you will be able to see significant weakness and neurological effects ranging from tremors to a feeling of paralysis (or even real paralysis).

The Origins of *Gelsemium*

Gelsemium sempervirens is one of the most beautiful native plants from the southern United States. According to Harvey Wickes Felter and John Uri Lloyd, authors of a nineteenth-century classic on medicinal herbs, *King's American Dispensatory*:

> *It is a twining vine, flourishing in great profusion from Virginia to Florida, hanging in festoons from the neighboring trees and shrubs, sometimes growing to the height of fifty feet. The average height, however, is from twenty to thirty feet. The plant blooms in early spring—in Florida during March, and in Mississippi and Tennessee in May and June. During the flowering period it perfumes the air with a delightful fragrance similar to that of the true jasmine. When the vine is abundant, the odor of the flowers is said to be almost overpowering.* [1]

Nicknamed false jasmine to distinguish it from true jasmine, which belongs to the family Oleacea, *Gelsemium* is classified as a member of the Loganacea family. Leafy and flowering parts of the plant are frequently used to decorate homes and gardens. However all parts of *Gelsemium sempervirens* are toxic, including the flower and the nectar. Highly poisonous, only its root is used in the preparation of the homeopathic remedy. True jasmine is native to Asia, not poisonous at all, and its flowers are used in jasmine tea and other herbal teas, and in blended black teas.

In 1753 the Carolina jessamine plant was originally identified and named *Bignonia sempervirens* by Swedish naturalist Carl Linnaeus. French botanist Antoine Laurent de Jussieu, whose subsequent work a few decades later piloted modern plant classification, renamed the genus in 1789. For this purpose, he changed the Italian word *gel-*

somino, meaning "jasmine," into its Latin form, *Gelsemium. Sempervirens* means "evergreen."

King's American Dispensatory offers the following description of the discovery of the medicinal qualities of *Gelsemium*:

> *This plant was brought into notice, as far as we can learn, in the following manner: A planter of Mississippi, whose name we have forgotten, while laboring under a severe attack of bilious fever, which resisted all the usual remedies, sent a servant into his garden to procure a certain medicinal root, and prepare an infusion of it for him to drink. The servant, by mistake, collected another root, and gave an infusion of it to his master, who, shortly after swallowing some of it, was seized with a complete loss of muscular power, unable to move a limb, or even raise his eyelids, although he could hear, and was cognizant of circumstances transpiring around him. His friends, greatly alarmed, collected around him, watching the result with much anxiety, and expecting every minute to see him breathe his last. After some hours, he gradually recovered himself, and was astonished to find that his fever had left him. Ascertaining from his servant what plant it was the root of which acted in this manner, he collected some of it, and employed it successfully on his own plantation, as well as among his neighbors. The success of this article finally reached the ear of some physician, who prepared from it a nostrum called the "Electrical Febrifuge," which was disguised with the essence of wintergreen. This plant was the yellow jessamine, and a knowledge of its remarkable effects was not communicated to the profession until a later period.*[2]

Those of you who read *National Geographic* or watch movies about Africa are probably noticing that the symptoms of yellow jasmine poisoning remind you of the effects of curare. You are correct. Curare and *Gelsemium* belong to the same family of plants. So do St. Ignatius's bean and Quaker buttons, the principle ingredients in the homeopathic remedies *Ignatia amara* and *Nux vomica*, covered in the next two chapters. Another important member of the same family, *Spigelia*, will make an appearance in this chapter when we talk about the treatment of headaches.

Believing this family of plants is unique because it has so many representatives among homeopathic remedies would be wrong. Numerous plant families provide important homeopathic remedies. This book would have to be a few thousand pages long to tell you about each and every one of them. Here we are presenting you with a few that can become your family's biggest allies in the course of everyday life.

The earliest descriptions of the homeopathic remedy prepared from *Gelsemium sempervirens* were published by American homeopaths in the 1850s and 1860s.

Symptoms Characteristic of the *Gelsemium* State

The key to understanding *Gelsemium* is that, when taken in its raw form, it affects the nervous system, and, as a result, the person feels intoxicated, weak, and paralyzed. Therefore, any condition that begins with the following unique set of symptoms can be helped with homeopathically prepared *Gelsemium*.

* Gradual onset (symptoms creep up on a person, like they do in cases of gradual paralysis)
* Intoxicated feeling, chills going up and down the spine, weakness and weariness, inability to think
* Feelings of apathy and wanting to be alone
* Stage fright (anticipation anxiety)
* Feelings of weakness and lethargy, perhaps with trembling from weakness
* Numbness
* Heavy eyelids that are difficult to open
* Heavy limbs
* Blurred vision
* Headache and heaviness, mostly in the back of the head

Conditions that trigger this combination of symptoms may include:

❋ Exposure to viruses
❋ Performance
❋ Neurological disorders (you need to see a neurologist as well as a homeopath to help these in the long run)

Things that improve the condition:

❋ Profuse perspiration or urination
❋ Vomiting
❋ Lying down with head high
❋ Alcohol (in cases of anxiety)
❋ Closing eyes

Things that make the condition worse:

❋ Heat
❋ Warm and wet weather
❋ Cold and damp weather
❋ Anticipation
❋ Lying down with head low

Acute Anxiety

Gelsemium is an excellent remedy for stage fright and test anxiety. People who need this remedy to perform better under various circumstances literally feel paralyzed, weak, and dizzy. They tremble and fear losing control. Their limbs become heavy. This is not a good bouquet of symptoms to have during performances or exams.

For students coping with test anxiety, I recommend first trying out *Gelsemium* on an occasion when the stakes are lower and consequences seem less important, such as before a weekly quiz rather than a midterm exam or a final. Imagine you were relying on a remedy to relieve your severe anxiety during an important test or a job interview, and it didn't work. That could trigger more anxiety.

If *Gelsemium* does not bring relief, the next important remedy to consider is *Argentum nitricum* (see description a little later in this section).

The protocol that I use is to take three pellets of *Gelsemium* 30C on the morning of the exam. I also prepare *Gelsemium* using the plussing method (see Chapter 2). The examinee takes a water bottle full of the diluted remedy to the test and sips from it as needed. You should not repeat the dose unless the anxiety begins to creep back on you. Each time you need to administer another dose, just shake the bottle again and drink about a teaspoon of the water. There's no need to add more pellets.

Exams are not the only anxiety-producing situation. Going on a date, especially for a shy person, can be an extreme emotional challenge. Another common cause of anxiety is public speaking. A few years ago, a family practice resident I was supervising told me that she felt so anxious speaking in public that she got weak and even trembled when she did. She asked for advice on what to do to prepare herself to give a wedding toast the next weekend. The miracle of *Gelsemium* turned her on to homeopathy.

If you have a tendency to become anxious or suffer from the anxiety disorder, a visit to a homeopath is a very good idea. On the other

Table 8.1 Acute Anxiety Remedy Comparison Chart

Remedy	Main Issues	Better From
Aconitum	Panic with no reason or after witnessing a horrible event; fear of doctors, dentists, surgery	Getting out of narrow place (bus, car, elevator)
Argentum nitricum	Anticipation anxiety (stage fright)	Motion; open air; company; talking
Gelsemium	Anticipation anxiety; terror before performance	Being alone

hand, I have seen cases when one-time use of *Gelsemium* or one of the following alternative remedies solved the issue of anxiety. Just be honest with yourself. If your problem continues, seek professional help.

Following are two other frequently indicated alternatives for cases of acute anxiety.

Aconitum napellus (monkshood).

* ❋ Panic with fear of death
* ❋ Sudden panic attacks
* ❋ Loss of control and extreme restlessness
* ❋ Need to get out now (for example, from an elevator or a subway car)
* ❋ Hyperventilation with tingling and numbness in the body
* ❋ Hot feeling

Argentum nitricum (silver nitrate). This remedy is easily confused with *Gelsemium*. Some experts suggest distinguishing the need for this remedy on the basis of diarrhea or other physical symptoms. Unfortunately, it is not always easy. However, there are certain features that make the correct choice possible. Whereas someone in a

Worse From	Guiding Signs	Remedy to Compare With
Narrow places; big crowds	Severe panic with fear of imminent death; loss of control; restlessness; feeling of being hot	*Argentum*
Warmth; being indoors	Hurried, nervous, always hot; desire for company and talking; afraid to be late; impulsive; has a sweet tooth	*Aconitum; Gelsemium*
Bad news; company	Timid; reserved; wants to be quiet	*Argentum*

Gelsemium state feels paralyzed from anxiety, an *Argentum nitricum* state is driven by anxiety on every level, including anxious diarrhea. People in a *Gelsemium* state want to be left alone. Those who need *Argentum nitricum* seek company and like to talk.

My advice to you in the case of stage fright is when in doubt, start with *Gelsemium*.

Characteristic symptoms of *Argentum nitricum* are:

* Hurriedness and nervousness
* Fears of being late, closed spaces, and heights (sometimes with impulse to jump)
* Desire for company and talking
* Sweet tooth
* Better: from motion and open air
* Worse: from warmth and being indoors

Fatigue and Weakness

Most of us have been tired at some point in our lives. If the feeling of exhaustion is a result of not having enough sleep, working too hard, or not eating well, these issues must be addressed. Homeopathy won't help. Stimulants might keep you up a bit longer, but ultimately you'll have to get enough sleep, food, and rest if you want to feel better.

Another side of exhaustion and fatigue is a possible underlying illness, such as mononucleosis, Lyme disease, diabetes, liver disorders, and thyroid conditions. The list of possibilities may go on and on. The bottom line is that you should seek rest, sleep, and food if there has been a lack of them. If there hasn't been such a deficit, or if you don't feel restored soon after taking self-care measures, go see a physician. In cases when the reason for exhaustion is identified and it isn't due to a significant illness, *Gelsemium* may be of great assistance.

Gelsemium should be considered if fatigue sets in after a viral infection and also in cases of feeling weak from fear, anticipation, or prolonged mental effort (compare with *Picricum acidum*). A person who needs *Gelsemium* feels drowsy and dull and has muscular weakness and trembling. The back of the head and limbs feel heavy. This individual wants to be left alone—completely alone. Even a quiet person is unwelcome in the same room. The condition is made worse by heat.

Following are six other frequently helpful remedies for fatigue and weakness. You'll notice that the last three are acids. Homeopathic remedies made from acids share one pronounced characteristic: they help reduce weakness from different types of causes. Every time a practitioner sees someone whose main complaint is weakness, the first possible remedy matches that come to mind are *Gelsemium* and the acids.

Of the most frequently indicated homeopathic acids, *Muriaticum acidum* is indicated mostly for people who experience physical weakness, *Phosphoricum acidum* for those who become weak and feel indifferent after enduring a severe emotional strain, such as grief, and *Picricum acidum* for people who feel weak after prolonged intellectual strain, such as cramming for exams or finishing a book.

Please remember that a person who becomes extremely weak after hearing bad news most probably needs *Gelsemium*. In cases such as these, you'll also see all the other typical identifying characteristics of the state, including a headache.

Let's look at the six common alternatives to *Gelsemium* now.

Arsenicum album (arsenic trioxide).

* Weakness with anxiety and restlessness
* Chill
* Burning pains that are better from heat
* Extreme fastidiousness, organized in a kind of neurotic, anxious way
* Insecurity and fear of death
* Thirst for small sips of cold water
* Better: from heat and company (someone in a *Gelsemium* state wants to be left alone)
* Worse: from cold and alcohol (compare with *Gelsemium*, which is better from alcohol)

Table 8.2 Fatigue and Weakness Remedy Comparison Chart

Remedy	Better	Worse
Arsenicum	Heat; company	Cold; alcohol
Carbo vegetabilis	Fanning	Stuffy room
China	Open air; warmth	Slightest touch; eating; night
Gelsemium	Profuse urination; open air; continued motion	Time preceding a thunderstorm; damp weather; excitement; 10 A.M.
Muriaticum acidum	Lying on the left side	Lying on the right side; sea bathing
Phosphoricum acidum	Keeping warm; juicy fruit	Being talked to; sex; loss of vital fluids
Picricum acidum	Cold air; cold water	Even the slightest mental exertion

Carbo vegetabilis (vegetable charcoal).

❁ Fainting in public places due to being exhausted
❁ Need for fresh air
❁ Better: from fanning and direct flow from air conditioning

Emotional State	Signs Guiding Your Selection	Remedy to Compare With
Anxious; restless; afraid of illnesses and death	Insecurity combined with fastidiousness; neurotic behavior; thirst for small sips of cold water	*China; Gelsemium*
Disoriented	Fainting in public places from exhaustion	*China; Gelsemium*
Sensitive to noise; touchy; afraid of animals (even pets); has many thoughts at night before going to sleep	Exhaustion after massive blood loss or any other fluid loss (e.g., prolonged diarrhea)	*Gelsemium*
Timid; reserved; wants to be alone	Weakness that increases gradually; difficulties opening the eyes	*China; Phosphoricum; Muriaticum*
Simply exhausted; no specific emotional features	Weakness that is purely physical; extreme crabbiness and weakness; involuntary stool while urinating	*Gelsemium; Phosphoricum*
Grieving; forgetful after grief; indifferent; lifeless; apathetic; feels dead inside	Weakness from grief or after a prolonged illness (e.g., mononucleosis)	*China; Gelsemium; Muriaticum*
Aversion to thinking, talking, or doing anything at all; often says, "I can't think"	Exhaustion after intense mental work (e.g., cramming for exams or finishing a project or a book)	*Phosphoricum*

China (*Cinchona officinalis*).

❋ Extreme exhaustion after blood loss, anemia, or prolonged illness

❋ Periodic symptoms (every hour, every day, every other day, and so on)

❈ Acute senses, hypersensitivity to touch or even a current of air, but with good tolerance for continuous pressure
❈ Vertigo
❈ Tinnitus (various sounds in the ear)
❈ Bitter taste in the mouth (even food that is desired tastes bitter)
❈ Worse: from motion

Muriaticum acidum (hydrochloric acid). This is considered one of the best remedies for typhoid fever, which is characterized by severe weakness.

❈ Weakness on the physical rather than the emotional level, exhaustion from clear physical reasons
❈ Severe weakness after, or even during, a long illness, along with high temperature
❈ Extreme crabbiness and weakness
❈ Involuntary stool when passing urine
❈ Protruding hemorrhoids
❈ Worse: from lying down on the right side and sea bathing

Phosphoricum acidum (phosphoric acid).

❈ Weakness from grief
❈ Forgetfulness and mental weakness after grief
❈ Weakness after a prolonged illness (for example, mononucleosis or prolonged diarrhea) or drug and alcohol abuse
❈ Lifelessness and apathy, as if dead inside
❈ Graying or even loss of hair after grief
❈ Craving for fruit, juices, and refreshing foods
❈ Paradoxically, possible profuse diarrhea without expected weakness

Picricum acidum (picric acid).

❈ Exhaustion after long studies (for example, cramming for exams) or prolonged intellectual strain
❈ Indifference

❈ Aversion to doing anything, even thinking or talking (frequently people in this state say, "I cannot think")

Headaches and Migraines

Treatment of chronic cluster and migraine headaches is a definite forte of homeopathy. The remedies in this section will help to eliminate your pain during an acute headache or the worsening of a chronic condition. But if your goal is to cure your headaches, rather than manage or ease them, it will be best to consult a homeopath. The reason some remedies are listed here is that these have clear and unique characteristics. If you happen to know someone whose headaches include these symptoms, or if these symptoms are characteristic of your own headaches, you are fortunate indeed. A remedy taken for acute pain may wind up curing the entire problem.

Following are a few things that a migraine or headache sufferer must consider in addition to homeopathy:

❈ Food allergies have been shown to be one of the major triggers of migraine headaches.[3] Undergoing the process of an elimination diet for a few weeks can help you to understand whether you are suffering from food allergies. To do an elimination diet, remove individual foods from your diet for a period of time, such as a week, and then return to eating them in a large quantity for one day. If you are sensitive to the particular food, you will experience noticeable symptoms then.

❈ Some people benefit from eating regular meals and abstaining from coffee.

❈ Feverfew is a popular herbal treatment for headaches.[4] Some people swear by it, and research has shown it to be effective.[5] Feverfew does not interfere with homeopathic treatment.

❈ Other effective nonhomeopathic measures for treating headaches include craniosacral therapy[6] and acupuncture. Some homeopaths (yours truly included) feel that acupuncture interferes with homeopathic treatment.

❊ Many headache sufferers routinely take three to four tablets of aspirin, acetaminophen (for example, Tylenol), or ibuprofen (for example, Motrin or Advil) for each episode of a headache. Be forewarned that there is a phenomenon known as a rebound headache, in which a vicious cycle is created of headache–medication–rebound headache–more medication and so on.

❊ If somebody who has never or rarely had a headache suddenly develops a severe headache, a full medical workup is indicated as soon as possible. The same is true for someone who develops repeated headaches. Go see the doctor. Better safe than sorry.

Gelsemium helps severe, exhausting headaches that show these signs:

❊ Heaviness in the head (especially if it begins in the back and extends to the forehead) or a sensation of having a tight band around the head
❊ Difficulty holding the head straight
❊ Difficulty opening the eyes
❊ Blurred vision or double vision during the headache
❊ Severe weakness with trembling during the headache
❊ Better: from urination (especially profuse urination) and lying down with head elevated
❊ Worse: at 10 A.M. and from lying flat

Following are additional remedies for acute headaches.

Arnica montana (leopard's bane). This remedy should always be considered first for headaches after head trauma.

❊ Desire to be left alone
❊ Better: from lying down with head low
❊ Worse: from waking up until 10 A.M.

Calcarea phosphorica (calcium phosphate). If this is the right remedy, I recommend using a cell salt in 6X potency.

Instructions: take three to five tablets two to three times a day for a month.

Important characteristics are:

❋ Headaches (in schoolchildren) that come after lunch or at
  the end of the school day
❋ Headache usually combined with a stomachache

China (*Cinchona officinalis*).

❋ Headaches after a serious loss of fluids (as happens during
  prolonged menopausal bleeding, breast-feeding, bouts
  of diarrhea, or such as are associated with anemia, for
  example)
❋ Weakness
❋ Pain in the whole head and going into the teeth
❋ Paleness during the headache
❋ Feeling that the brain hits the walls of the inside of the skull
❋ Better: from hard pressure with the hand, warm room, and
  moving head up and down
❋ Worse: from open air, drafts, noise, motion, and even touch

Cocculus indicus (Indian cockle).

❋ Headache from many worries and loss of sleep (as happens
  when taking care of a loved one who is very ill, for example)
❋ Headache with dizziness, nausea, and vomiting (which is
  possibly triggered by noise)
❋ Pain that is frequently located in the back of the head
  (compare with *Gelsemium*) but can also be in the whole head
❋ Better: from sleep and lying on one side or the other
❋ Worse: from riding as a passenger in a car and from loss
  of sleep

Ignatia amara (St. Ignatius's bean).

❋ Headache caused by bad news (for example, a breakup) and
  grief
❋ Headache with back or neck spasms
❋ Pain that feels like a nail was stuck in the side of the head

Nux vomica (Quaker buttons).

❀ Tension headaches as a result of a hangover, toxic headaches
❀ Oversensitivity to all stimuli
❀ Irritability and anger
❀ Constipation during headache
❀ Better: from warm applications and lying on the painless side
❀ Worse: from cold, stimuli (for example, noise, odor, light, or wind), motion, eating, and lying on the painful side (compare with *Bryonia*)

Table 8.3 General Headaches and Migraines Remedy Comparison Chart

Remedy	Better	Worse
Arnica	Lying down with head low	Waking up until 10 A.M.
Calcarea phosphorica	Warm, dry weather	Change of weather; after lunch or the end of the day
China	Hard pressure with hand; moving head up and down; warm room; hot weather	Lying flat; 10 A.M.
Cocculus	Sleep; lying on the side (takes pressure off the back of the head)	Loss of sleep; riding in a car; lying on the back; pressure on the back of the head
Gelsemium	Urination; lying down with head elevated	Time preceding a thunderstorm; damp weather; excitement; 10 A.M.
Ignatia	Lying on painful side; alcohol; motion; warm applications	Emotions; being in a room where other people smoke
Nux vomica	Warm applications; lying on the painless side; morning (rising from bed)	Cold; alcohol; noise; light; morning in bed

Right-Sided Headaches and Migraines

Our discussion would not be complete if we did not address remedies helpful for pain on a particular side of the head. Following are five remedies for right-sided headache pain.

Belladonna (deadly nightshade).

* ❋ Headache that starts or disappears suddenly (sometimes both)
* ❋ Extremely painful, pulsating headache (sufferer may report that the pain is exploding or maddening)

Emotional State	Signs Guiding Your Selection	Remedy to Compare With
Wants to be left alone	Headaches after head trauma	
Peevish; always wants change, to go somewhere	Headaches in schoolchildren	
Sensitive to noise; touchy	Headaches after significant fluid loss (prolonged bleeding, prolonged diarrhea, etc.) or anemia	*Gelsemium*
Sensitive and sympathetic; anxious about loved ones	Headaches from worries (e.g., as a result of taking care of a sick relative or friend)	*Gelsemium*
Timid; reserved; wants to be alone	Heaviness that begins in the back of the head and travels to the forehead; difficulties opening the eyes	*China; Cocculus*
Easily hurt; easily offended; may be hysterical	Headaches after grief, divorce, or breakup; pain that feels like a nail was stuck in the side of the head	*Cocculus*
Irritable and very easily offended (characteristics are magnified during the headache)	Headaches from hangover, drug abuse, and tension; migraine headaches	*Ignatia*

❀ Sensation that the brain is pressing outward (sufferer may say, "It feels like my eyes will pop out")

❀ Headache that begins in the back of the head and either extends from the back to the right side, or goes all the way to the right forehead and/or the right eye

❀ Large pupils

❀ Hot head and flushed face but cold hands and/or feet

❀ Better: from lying down in a quiet, dark room

❀ Worse: from motion, light, noise, stooping, and washing hair

Cedron (cedron seed).

❀ Pain that returns at exactly the same time (same hour every day, every three days, weekly, monthly, or so forth)

Table 8.4 Right-Sided Headaches Remedy Comparison Chart

Remedy	Better	Worse
Belladonna	Lying in a quiet, dark room	Light; sound
Cedron	No modalities	Rising; open air; 9 A.M. or 11 A.M.
Iris	Constant slow, relaxed motion; standing	Rest; sitting; cold air
Ranunculus	Standing or walking	Time preceding a storm; change of weather; alcohol
Sanguinaria	Vomiting; sleep or rest; pressing head against hard surfaces	Fasting; daytime (comes and goes with the sun)

❀ Swollen feeling in head
❀ Numb feeling in body

Iris versicolor (harlequin blue flag).

❀ Frequently, classical headaches that come on weekends
  or during rest
❀ Headache that begins with visual aura and ends with
  vomiting
❀ Blurry vision, sometimes even blindness (compare with
  Belladonna)
❀ Headache that may go from side to side
❀ Better: from walking, standing, and constant relaxed motion
❀ Worse: from rest, sitting, and cold air

Emotional State	Signs Guiding Your Selection	Remedy to Compare With
Acute senses; sensitive to light and sound	Extreme painfulness; maddening, pulsating headache (as if brain is pressing outward and as if the eyes will pop out)	*Iris*
No specific data	Pain that comes back at exactly the same hour (daily, every two days, or any periodicity); possible numbness of whole body along with the headache	*Sanguinaria*
No specific data	Classic migraine that begins with aura and ends with vomiting; blindness during the headache	*Belladonna*
Irritable	Headache that starts before a storm; headache that is much worse from alcohol (can be triggered by alcohol)	*Sanguinaria*
No specific data	Pain that begins in the back of the head, frequently in the neck and shoulder, and then goes into the eye; menopausal headaches; flushed face with pulsating carotids	*Belladonna*

Ranunculus bulbosus (St. Anthony's turnip).

❊ Headache before a storm
❊ Worse: (much worse) from alcohol

Sanguinaria canadensis (bloodroot).

❊ Headache that begins in the back of the head, or even the neck
   and right shoulder, and goes into the right eye
❊ Face flushed with pulsating carotids (compare carefully with
   Belladonna)
❊ Headache that appears with the sunrise and goes away with the
   sunset
❊ Vomiting during headaches
❊ Periodic headaches
❊ Better: from sleep and rest, after vomiting, and from pressing
   head against hard surfaces
❊ Worse: during daytime and from light, noise, odors, fasting,
   jarring, and menses

Table 8.5 Left-Sided Headaches Remedy Comparison Chart

Remedy	Better	Worse
Bryonia	Immobilization; pressure; lying on the painful side	The slightest motion (even of the eyes or closing and opening eyelids)
Sepia	Vigorous exercise; eating	Time before and/or during menses; sex (in contrast to most people who report improvement of headaches during sex)
Spigelia	Heat (e.g., a hot bath); lying down with head elevated and eyes closed	Any exertion, even straining to pass a stool; jarring; cold, open air

Left-Sided Headaches

To balance out the last section, following are three remedies specifically for left-sided headache pain.

Bryonia alba (white bryony).

* Bursting headache that begins over the left eye and goes into the back of the head and may spread to the entire head
* Headache that starts in the morning or at 9 P.M.
* Better: from pressure (because nothing can move) and lying on the painful side (same idea of not moving)
* Worse: from even a slight motion (like moving the eyes or closing and opening eyelids)

Sepia (cuttlefish ink).

* Headache in the left forehead or above the left eye (compare with *Spigelia*)

Emotional State	Signs Guiding Your Selection	Remedy to Compare With
Irritable; wants to be alone	Pain that is much worse from motion; pain that begins over the left eye and goes into the back or spreads over the entire head	*Spigelia*
Wants to be alone	Better from exercise and eating; clearly worse around menses	*Spigelia*
Possibly afraid of sharp objects	Pain that is exactly above the left eye	*Bryonia; Sepia*

❉ "Sick headache" (that is, with nausea)
❉ Better: from vigorous exercise (compare with many other remedies—most are worse from motion) and eating
❉ Worse: before and/or during menses, from sex (by contrast,
most migraine sufferers report improvement during sex or mas-
turbation), and from artificial light

Spigelia (pinkroot).

❉ Headache above the left eye
❉ Violent pain in one spot that the sufferer can clearly point to
with one finger
❉ Pain that is like a stitch in the side
❉ Headache may be associated with heart palpitations or any
other heart problems
❉ Better: from heat, taking a hot bath, and lying down with ele-
vated head and closed eyes
❉ Worse: from jarring, any type of exertion (including straining to
pass a stool), cold, open air, wind, and smoke

A Few More Conditions That May Require *Gelsemium*

Some people develop significant signs of anxiety when they have diarrhea and show all the typical modalities of *Gelsemium* on those occasions. *Gelsemium* is also helpful in many cases of fever and, as you
already learned in Chapter 4, is one of the main remedies used for
the treatment of flu.

Romantic disappointment or grief ❊ Primarily helpful to females ❊ Any ailment that develops after grief (for example, menstrual problems, headache, digestive problems, paroxysmal cough without signs of illness, even physical pain) ❊ Lump in the throat ❊ Compulsion to sigh or yawn frequently ❊ Desire not to be comforted—preference to be alone ❊ Hysterical crying ❊ Tendency to be easily offended ❊ Hysteria and hysterical symptoms (for example, numbness, unexplainable paralysis after a significant emotional event, and so on) ❊ Symptoms that are exactly the opposite of what you would normally expect (for example, throat pain made better by swallowing)

9

Ignatia

Your Homeopathic Therapist

Where joy most revels, grief doth most lament;
Grief joys, joy grieves on slender accident.

—WILLIAM SHAKESPEARE, *Hamlet*

IGNATIA AMARA (St. Ignatius's bean, *Strychnos ignatii*) is one of the most commonly needed remedies for coping with grief and loss. It provides relief by healing emotional pain and physical complaints that result from bereavement. *Ignatia* is the right remedy for a person who feels that the situation he or she is mourning remains real, as if it happened yesterday, and continues constantly to focus on it.

The value of this remedy in modern society cannot be overestimated. It is used to treat both the initial stages and the long-term consequences of emotional crises, such as a divorce, a miscarriage, a sudden job loss, the death of a close friend, witnessing the devastation of war, or moving away from home. Today we are becoming ever more aware of the effects of various psychological issues like these, and going to a therapist is now as routine as visiting a local pastry shop was a hundred years ago. Therefore, we have more experience in overcoming such losses. *Ignatia* comes in handy in all these types of situations and can improve your resilience so you and your family members don't get stuck in the past.

How can you recognize the *Ignatia* state? *Ignatia* is a medication for grief and anguish. Among other traits, the person who needs this remedy has hysterical reactions, like prolonged crying jags and numbness. Another important feature of the state *Ignatia* cures is paradoxical behavior (for example, when an upset person refuses to be consoled and comforted) and counterintuitive symptoms (such as throat pain that is improved, rather than worsened, by the act of swallowing).

The Origins of *Ignatia*

Strychnos ignatii is a large, woody climbing shrub that produces large, extremely bitter fruit. Resembling a medium-sized pear, the fruit has seeds that are about an inch long. As you may have guessed, the fruit's bitterness is due to strychnine contained in the seeds, which makes them poisonous on one hand and of high medicinal value on the other. Homeopathic preparations of *Ignatia amara* are made from the seeds.

The plant is indigenous to the Philippine Islands, where the natives have long recognized its therapeutic properties. But instead of preparing potions from it, they wore the seeds as amulets for the prevention and cure of various diseases. Malaysians call *Ignatia amara upas paja*, meaning "royal poison," and historically used the juice of the fruit to poison their arrows for hunting, and occasionally for murdering their human enemies.

The Europeans learned about *Ignatia* from Spanish priests who named the shrub after the founder of the Jesuit order, St. Ignatius of Loyola. Jesuit priest George Kamel, a man who dedicated his life to natural science, collected the plant and introduced the seed known as St. Ignatius's bean to Europe in the latter half of the seventeenth century.

In 1818 French chemists Joseph-Bienaimé Caventou and Pierre-Joseph Pelletier discovered strychnine while studying the contents of St. Ignatius's bean. Interestingly, both *Ignatia amara* (*Strychnos ignatii*) and *Nux vomica*, a plant scientifically known as *Strychnos Nux-vomica* (see Chapter 10), contain strychnine and another alkaloid, brucine, although in different proportions. *Ignatia* contains one-third more strychnine and a lesser percentage of brucine than found in *Nux vomica*.

Dr. Hahnemann conducted the first proving of *Ignatia* and described it in great detail. As in the many other cases we've discussed, Hahnemann's discovery of the innovative homeopathic method for the preparation of remedies allowed him to extract the medicinal qualities of this amazing plant and neutralize its poisonous qualities.

Symptoms Characteristic of the *Ignatia* State

Many homeopathic authorities have written that *Ignatia* is the female counterpart of *Nux vomica*, a remedy for males. This comparison is tempting, because both remedies are derived from plants that belong to the same genus, *Strychnos*. The idea of male and female attributes complementing each other in nature has always been enticing to humankind. Although it may be true, the reality of the modern lifestyle is that in their normal daily existence, people—of both genders—who benefit from taking *Ignatia* are sensitive, easily excitable, "quick in perceiving, prompt in appreciation and rapid in execution."[1] These people are also highly idealistic and really don't appreciate contradiction.

As we all know, our era is characterized by globalization and integration. This trend certainly affects the way men and women think, feel, and behave. Contrary to the historical record, in my practice I have seen many men who benefited from *Ignatia* and many women who were cured by *Nux vomica*.

An even more important concept to appreciate is that at certain ages and under the influence of certain situations, people have a tendency to move into particular mental, emotional, and physical states. After reading this chapter, you'll be able to see that going through adolescence, being romantically involved, and losing a loved one all may move a person into the condition that can be remedied by *Ignatia*.

An essential detail to recognize is that people who need *Ignatia* feel as if they lost someone just a few hours earlier. The wound is still fresh. The emotional pain is acute—even if the loss happened a long time ago. It's as though whomever they are missing was just here and is only now gone. And the loss feels terribly unfair. The pain is practically unbearable.

Later in the chapter, when you read about the picture of *Natrum muriaticum*, *Ignatia*'s twin from the mineral kingdom, keep in mind that this sense of the loss as still being fresh and almost unbearably painful is the main feature that distinguishes the need for *Ignatia* from the need for *Natrum muriaticum*.

The state that requires *Ignatia* can best be described in one word: hysteria. According to one medical dictionary, hysteria is "behavior exhibiting excessive or uncontrollable emotion."[2] When people are hysterical, it doesn't mean they are exceedingly amused, as in laughing hysterically. Instead, it means they are feeling and acting out of control.

A lot of symptoms in the *Ignatia* state seem to be exactly the opposite of what you'd expect. For example, there may be a fever but no thirst, a sore throat that is improved by swallowing, sensitivity that is relieved by pressure, a chill offset by removing covers, a headache relieved by the act of bending forward, and so on. This tendency for reversal is so pronounced that Dr. A. L. Monroe, a prominent nineteenth-century British homeopath, once said, "One must look for the body of a drowned *Ignatia* patient 'up stream.'"

People who need *Ignatia* don't necessarily act crazy; rather, these individuals usually feel like things are going out of control and they must do everything they can to control themselves. Though not always successful in this regard, they sometimes do achieve control.

Let's look at prominent examples of symptoms caused by the effort to control oneself despite the feeling that things are falling apart, as a person might feel in the case of being abandoned by a loved one either due to death or a relationship breakup. Those who need *Ignatia* might:

❊ Have a globus hystericus, a medical term for feeling a lump in the throat
❊ Attempt to suppress crying and wind up sobbing
❊ Dislike sympathy and consolation, because those offering comfort might see how devastated they really are (teenagers, for instance, frequently run into their bedrooms, lock the door behind them, and then start crying uncontrollably)
❊ Sigh because the chest tightens up from their efforts to keep their emotions inside
❊ Experience numbness, or even temporary paralysis without a physical cause, also caused by trying to hold everything inside
❊ Have back spasms from stress-related tension after grief (do you get it now?)
❊ Be very defensive, touchy, and easily offended
❊ Want to travel and feel much better when traveling (they have a desire to escape and not to show their real emotions)

Circumstances that trigger this combination of symptoms may include:

❊ The death of a loved one or a companion animal
❊ A breakup or divorce
❊ A miscarriage
❊ Being the victim of a violent act, such as an assault, rape, or robbery
❊ Being the victim of an accident or another scary event
❊ For children, watching their parents fighting or getting a divorce
❊ Homesickness
❊ Unfair treatment
❊ Being fired from a job

Let's talk about specific situations in which *Ignatia* and a few other remedies can be of great help. You may notice that there are only a few additional remedies described here, fewer than in most other chapters. The reason is simple: the emotional core is the most complicated and sophisticated part of the human being. Only a few remedies with the most obvious symptoms are appropriate for self-care. Fortunately, these are the remedies people often tend to need. More complicated grieving situations should be treated by an experienced homeopath, and it is highly desirable to involve a mental health professional in the treatment team.

Emotional Crisis and Grief

As a qualified psychiatrist and homeopath, in my medical practice I've had to prescribe *Ignatia* on numerous occasions. The following two case studies will serve to illustrate the key symptoms and remarkable curative power of this great remedy.

Once I treated a young woman suffering from bipolar disorder. In the initial interview to evaluate her, she told me she wasn't doing well on her conventional medications and therefore was looking to improve the quality of her life using complementary methods of treatment. After an hour together, it was clear that my patient needed *Ignatia* for constitutional treatment of her condition. Before she left, I gave her a dose of three pellets of *Ignatia amara* 200C, and we decided to meet again a month later.

Our follow-up appointment started with the woman describing how amazingly easy it was for her to tolerate her latest breakup. Her boyfriend of more than a year had ended their relationship three days after our first meeting. Prior to taking *Ignatia*, breakups like this one—even those that she initiated—were always devastating to my patient and would send her into a deep depression. This time, she reported, "I was hurt, but it was more on the intellectual, rather than emotional, level. I was absolutely fine!"

I have had to prescribe *Ignatia* for broken hearts on many occasions. It does miracles both prophylactically and after the event, but only under one condition: that the person who takes it is demonstrating typical symptoms of this remedy. Taking *Ignatia* before a traumatic event works only for people—usually girls and women—who have a tendency to suffer at the end of relationships. Still, it is worth keeping *Ignatia amara* 200C on hand just in case it is ever needed.

Another situation where *Ignatia* is frequently of great help is when a person experiences grief following a death. I have lost a few people with whom I was close in my life. So far, the most painful experience was the death of my eighty-seven-year-old father. But I didn't need the remedy—my mother did. Taking *Ignatia* literally changed her entire attitude, not only immediately after the fact but also when we went to visit the grave for the first time after the burial. A few other elderly women who came along on this occasion also benefited greatly.

Instructions: take all remedies for emotional crisis and grief in concentration 200C, three pellets at a time. *Ignatia amara* 200C can be taken as needed for the duration of an emotional crisis, provided that it produces the effect of lessening the severity of your emotional strain. *Ignatia* is the most useful homeopathic remedy for coping with acute grief, and it is indicated in a large proportion of cases.

Of course, *Ignatia* is far from a one-size-fits-all proposition. Following you will find descriptions of two other remedies that are frequently required for emotional crises and grief. Always compare *Ignatia* with *Natrum muriaticum* and, especially, *Phosphoricum acidum*. If you are having the correct symptoms, I recommend taking either *Natrum muriaticum* or phosphoric acid only once, a dose of three 200C pellets. These remedies are long acting and will work just fine after a single dose.

If you happen to take a dose or two of the wrong remedy when you're in an emotional crisis, no harm will be done; however, it is a good idea to proceed with seeing a professional homeopath in order to gain some relief. There is no need to suffer.

Following are the two main alternate remedies for emotional crises and grief.

Natrum muriaticum (sodium chloride). The picture of this remedy can be difficult to distinguish from *Ignatia*. But there is one major distinction: people who need *Ignatia* are usually idealistic and trusting and have high energy. If something bad happens, they are disillusioned and totally unprepared for the loss and therefore go into the *Ignatia* state. As I mentioned before, *Ignatia* is indicated when the loss feels as if it happened only a few hours earlier or like it was just yesterday. People needing *Natrum muriaticum* are different. They are born to be sensitive to any loss. It is their nature to look back into the past. For this reason, homeopaths frequently use the biblical story of Lot's wife from Genesis as a metaphor for people who need *Natrum muriaticum*.

As the story goes, God gave Lot and his immediate family an opportunity to escape the destruction of Sodom and Gomorrah. The only stipulation of their salvation was that they weren't allowed to watch—only to flee. Despite this warning, Lot's wife glanced backward over her shoulder and was transformed into a pillar of salt. What is the raw material of *Natrum muriaticum*? Sodium chloride, or table salt!

Natrum muriaticum is usually beneficial to people who've been exposed to many losses. More importantly, those who need this remedy are extremely sensitive to loss, as someone relocating to a new town might feel or a teenager whose friends were going to a different school might feel. Another important tendency of people who need this remedy is that they try to keep everything inside. They do it more successfully than people who need *Ignatia*. Such a person is reserved, proper, and quiet even at an early age.

The chief characteristics of *Natrum muriaticum* are the following:

* Behavior that is too serious (for example, children who are too serious for their age), proper, and extremely responsible
* Much relief—relaxation, laughter—from imbibing alcoholic drinks (this trait might lead to alcoholism and drug abuse)
* Depression but without the ability to cry
* Tendency to be easily offended and hurt

- ❊ Inclination to giggle while talking about sad stories (for example, a girl who describes being abused by her mother and giggles as if it is funny)
- ❊ Tendency for dwelling on past losses and humiliations
- ❊ Perfectionism, dresses very neatly (even children)
- ❊ Tendency to be easily moved by music (to both tears and laughter) and to love music
- ❊ No tolerance for exposure to the sun
- ❊ Migraine headaches
- ❊ Cold sores on the lips and, especially, inside the mouth
- ❊ Back pain (frequently in the lower back) that is much improved from lying on a hard surface (for example, a floor)
- ❊ Craving for salt

In an article in *Homeopathy Today*, the periodic journal of the National Center for Homeopathy, Todd A. Hoover, M.D., a homeopath based in Philadelphia, Pennsylvania, described the type of person needing *Natrum muriaticum* well: "these individuals are literally swollen with grief."[3] That sense of emotional swelling frequently translates into physical problems, which, for instance, might include severe migraine headaches. *Natrum muriaticum* relieves such ailments.

We shouldn't underestimate the power a single dose of the right remedy can have on us—or on other living creatures. Homeopath Jack Lawyer told me the true story of Seri, a young elephant living in the Rosamond Gifford Zoo in Syracuse, New York.[4] She had a happy relationship with her keeper, Chuck, and frolicked happily in her enclosure until he got promoted and couldn't have close contact with her anymore. This was a great shock to her. You could easily compare the impact this decision had on the elephant with the trauma people experience when they watch close relatives accidentally die. As a result of Chuck's transfer, Seri experienced symptoms typical of post-traumatic stress disorder or depression: the elephant lost interest in activities, developed severe physical symptoms that included pain and swelling in her legs and ulcers on her ankles, and became irritable and angry. Her appetite also was poor. Seri was so sad that she gradually withdrew and wouldn't interact with anyone. It enraged her if people tried to break into her solitude.

Zoo staff called veterinarians numerous times, but all their efforts to treat Seri using conventional veterinary medicine were in vain. The grief-stricken young elephant continued to suffer. In fact, she was dying. Finally, the staff saw only one way to relieve Seri of her misery: she would have to be put down.

Although Anne Baker, the executive director of the zoo, didn't believe in homeopathy, she was a good friend of Jack, knew about his studies of homeopathy, and decided to ask him what they could do as a last resort. Jack visited Seri. He noticed many important things about this elephant and gave her a dose of *Natrum muriaticum* 1M. This single dose of the remedy brought Seri back to life. After its administration, she began gradually improving and soon returned to being a happy elephant. Jack visited Seri many times, but he never saw the need to give her another dose of the remedy.

Phosphoricum acidum (phosphoric acid). The best description I've ever heard of the emotional state that requires this remedy was offered by eminent American homeopath Paul Herscu. Imagine a

Table 9.1 Emotional Crisis and Grief Remedy Comparison Chart

Remedy	Better	Worse
Ignatia	Traveling	Consolation
Natrum muriaticum	Alcohol; going without regular meals	Consolation; talking
Phosphoricum acidum	No data	Being talked to

dog that lived with its owner for many years. One day the owner takes the dog to the airport, sits it in the corner, gets on a plane, and flies away forever. Meanwhile, the dog just sits there in total despair and waits. It doesn't move. It doesn't eat. It is so overwhelmed by the loss that it is simply unable to respond to anything else.

Like this sorrowful dog that has been so grievously abandoned, the person needing *Phosphoricum acidum* feels completely drained of energy. The person is apathetic, enervated, and bone tired. In essence, the person feels dead. Someone can develop the state that requires this remedy as a result of loss or physical illnesses like mononucleosis or chronic diarrhea. In addition, alcohol and drug abuse frequently lead to a similar state.

Here are important characteristics of the remedy:

* ❊ Apathy
* ❊ Forgetfulness, tendency to get lost easily, and, frequently, development of problems with memory after grief
* ❊ Indifference (frequently just sits or lies around all day)
* ❊ Craving for juicy fruit, fruit juices, and refreshing drinks
* ❊ Better: from sleep, even if it is a short nap

Emotional State	Signs Guiding Your Selection	Remedy to Compare With
Romantic disappointment, grief; defensive; touchy; easily offended	Grief that is very much on the surface (regardless of real time); tendency to be easily hurt and offended; possibly, rudeness and suspiciousness; sighing and sobbing	*Natrum muriaticum*
Reserved; very responsible; reliable	Sadness but with inability to cry; inclination to giggle while talking about very sad events; tendency to be easily moved by music; tendency for dwelling on past occurrences; craving for salt	*Ignatia*
Apathetic; feels frozen and dead inside	Depression; apathy; lifelessness; exhaustion due to grief	*Ignatia; Natrum muriaticum*

Depression

On its own, any medication, even a powerful homeopathic remedy, cannot resolve the multiple issues a depressed person has. Combining homeopathy and psychotherapy is a significantly more beneficial approach. Of course, it is easier said than done if you decide to locate a psychiatrist who also knows homeopathy. My credentials, which unite these professions, are rare. However, if such a combination is not available near you, first connect with a good psychiatrist and then seek homeopathic help separately. Never attempt to treat depression yourself. Always seek help from a mental health professional.

Having said that, I feel compelled to mention one remedy, as it is the most helpful remedy for suicidal depression. Without a doubt, a suicidal person must be hospitalized—right away. After you hang up the phone with emergency services, give the suicidal person three pellets of *Aurum metallicum* (gold) 200C, 1M, or 10M. Then don't leave the side of the person until professional help arrives.

Why would I recommend a homeopathic remedy if the person is going to the hospital? Because there is no conventional medication that treats the urge to commit suicide. In fact, the FDA issued recent warnings about the increase of suicidal behavior due to the use of conventional antidepressants. Although *Aurum metallicum* isn't the only possible remedy for suicidal people, it is the most frequently indicated one. It will do its job in the long run. I've seen it work many times.

Warning: never leave a suicidal person alone, even if this person wants to go to the bathroom. It is imperative to stand by and watch over him or her until help arrives.

An alternative to calling an ambulance and waiting for its arrival is to give the suicidal person the remedy and take that person to the emergency room. Bottom line: a suicidal individual has to be taken to the hospital for professional observation.

Insomnia

According to some estimates, one in eight people, or thirty-two million Americans, suffer from insomnia.[5] Regardless of how accurate this estimate is, we all know that many people have difficulties falling asleep and maintaining sleep. In my experience, professional constitutional treatment of insomnia can be successful if it is combined with better sleep hygiene and relaxation techniques. In new cases of insomnia, you also have to make sure that there are no serious underlying health problems.

Lack of sleep is not a trivial matter. We all know how difficult it is to function if we don't get enough quality sleep each night. Yet it is not easy to treat insomnia. Insomnia is frequently a segment of a vicious cycle of a more serious disease. For example, a loss of sleep in someone's late teens or early twenties could be a sign of emerging bipolar disorder or clinical depression. Or it could be the result of an abnormally functioning thyroid gland. Or it could be the result of severe stress at work. Obviously, I could go on and on.

When insomnia is a result of easily identified factors, a few herbal remedies, such as hops (tea or extract) and valerian root, can be soothing. In my experience, melatonin also provides significant relief for mild insomnia. If insomnia persists or it is already a chronic problem, you should have a thorough medical workup and consult an experienced homeopath for constitutional treatment.

Following are several homeopathic remedies that can be helpful in cases of simple, easy-to-understand insomnia. Anything beyond that really belongs in the realm of what a trained homeopath can offer. *Ignatia* is appropriate for treating insomnia that's the result of grief, a breakup, or bad news.

Main characteristics to look for in cases of insomnia that respond to *Ignatia* include:

* Fear that the patient won't be able to fall asleep ever again
* Changeable moods
* Waking up crying
* Frequent nervous yawning and sighing
* Jerking of limbs on going to sleep

Compare *Ignatia* with the following remedies. (*Instructions:* it is best to take one dose of any remedy you select in concentration 200C, with the exception of *Calcarea phosphorica*.)

Arnica montana (leopard's bane). This is for insomnia after a recent accident or jet lag. Main indicators of needing this remedy are:

❊ Nightmares or vivid dreams of an accident and injuries that the person had
❊ Feeling of being extremely tired but with inability to sleep
❊ Feeling of being bruised, with the bed feeling too hard

Calcarea phosphorica (calcium phosphate). This is for insomnia in children going through growth spurts or for insomnia after a long illness.

Instructions: give three to five tablets of a cell salt in potency 6X two to three times a day for a month.

Major indicators are:

❊ Discontent and constant complaining (compare with *Chamomilla*)
❊ Feeling of still being tired in the morning even after a long sleep
❊ Tension in the neck and shoulders

Chamomilla (German chamomile). This is for insomnia triggered by the overuse of coffee or drugs, pain, or sleeplessness in children due to teething and/or colic.

Major characteristics are:

❊ Drowsiness during the day and sleeplessness at night
❊ Irritability, capriciousness, being demanding
❊ Desire (of child) to be carried all the time
❊ Crying and moaning in sleep (to be considered only in combination with other symptoms)

China (*Cinchona officinalis*). This is for insomnia after loss of fluids, such as from bleeding, prolonged breast-feeding, profuse sweating, or diarrhea.

Signs of this remedy are:

❊ Many thoughts running in the head, preventing a person from falling asleep
❊ Extreme sensitivity (especially to noise)

***Cocculus indicus* (Indian cockle).**

❊ Sleeplessness from exhaustion brought about by night vigils (such as sitting up with a sick relative)
❊ Waking up startled
❊ Confirmation for this remedy is that patient gets motion sickness

***Coffea cruda* (unroasted coffee).** This is the most frequently used homeopathic remedy for temporary relief of insomnia.

Note: do not be tempted to offer this remedy to coffee drinkers, because *Chamomilla* is the right remedy for the abuse of caffeine.

Use this remedy for:

❊ Insomnia from excitement and too much enthusiasm
❊ Head full of ideas
❊ Difficulty falling asleep because of excitement and many thoughts
❊ Extreme sensitivity to pain, touch, light, odors, and sounds
❊ High nervous energy, even hyperactivity

***Gelsemium sempervirens* (yellow jasmine).** This remedy offers significant relief in cases of insomnia that are secondary to anticipation, overwork, overstudying, and also colds, the flu, mononucleosis, and a difficult pregnancy. Use it when you see these signs:

❊ Heavy head, especially in the back
❊ Mental dullness

✣ Weakness
✣ Tendency to fall asleep in the evening after supper or while watching TV or studying and then to wake up an hour or two later unable to go back to sleep

Table 9.2 Insomnia Remedy Comparison Chart

Remedy	Reason for Insomnia
Arnica	Jet lag; recent accident
Calcarea phosphorica	Growth spurt (in children)
Chamomilla	Teething; colic; overuse of coffee; pain
China	Significant bleeding; prolonged breast-feeding; prolonged diarrhea; malaria
Cocculus	Night vigils (e.g., sitting up with a sick relative)
Coffea	Excitement
Gelsemium	Anticipation (like before a test or important presentation); flu; mononucleosis
Ignatia	Grief; bad news
Nux vomica	Abuse of alcohol, stimulants, or street drugs; overwork and stress; working too hard and playing too hard

Nux vomica (Quaker buttons). This is often the remedy of choice for insomnia from anger, abuse of stimulants and drugs, and drinking too much alcohol or overeating the night before. It is also used for insomnia caused by overwork and stress—the typical businessperson's lifestyle.

Emotional State	Physical Symptoms, Modalities
Has vivid dreams or nightmares of an accident or injury	Extreme exhaustion with bruised feeling; bed feels hard
Discontented; constantly complaining	Shifting pains in the bones; exhaustion in the morning even after a long sleep; tension in the neck and shoulders
Irritable; demanding; crying and moaning in sleep; child wants to be carried	Sleepy during the day but cannot sleep at night
Sensitive to noise; irritable; has many thoughts running through the head at night	Feeling of being very cold and weak
Worried about relatives or friends in need	Motion sickness; wakes up startled
Has high nervous energy; full of many thoughts and ideas	Very acute senses (to pain, touch, light, odors, sounds)
Mentally dull	Falls asleep in the early evening just to wake up in a few hours and not be able to go back to sleep; weakness with heaviness in the back of the head
Fearful of never falling asleep again; wakes up crying	Frequent nervous yawning and sighing; jerking of limbs on going to sleep
Irritable; angry; always on the edge; irritated by noises	Wakes up around 3 A.M. full of thoughts about work and problems

Look for signs like:

* The tendency to fall asleep early and then wake up at 3 A.M., full of thoughts about problems
* Irritability and anger
* Irritation from noises or any other interference

A Few More Conditions That May Require *Ignatia*

As you may imagine, any condition with contradictory symptoms that develops in a person with a history of grief or significant loss could respond beautifully to *Ignatia*. A homeopath acquaintance of mine, for example, couldn't figure out a remedy for a patient's mastitis (breast infection) and then learned that the woman had lost a close and beloved relative a year earlier. After the homeopath gave her patient one dose of *Ignatia*, the mastitis disappeared. Now obviously, this homeopath was experienced and ran numerous possible solutions through her head before she resorted to prescribing *Ignatia*. If she'd seen any symptoms of a more frequently used remedy for mastitis, she would have tried that first.

FOCUS POINTS

Irritability and anger ❁ High sensitivity to all external stimuli ❁ Extreme
sensitivity to cold ❁ Most symptoms improve with warmth

10

Nux Vomica

Your Homeopathic Gastroenterologist

*You don't get ulcers from what you eat. You get them
from what's eating you.*

—VICKI BAUM

EVERY HOMEOPATH in the world prescribes *Nux vomica* (Quaker buttons, poison nut, *Strychnos nux-vomica*) very frequently. The reason underlying such common use of this medication is simple: it is perfectly suited to the emotional and physical state triggered by the typical stressors of the modern lifestyle. Even in this short book, you've already "met" *Nux vomica* when potential remedies were being compared for insomnia and headaches. The individual who needs it feels stressed out and overworked.

Just for a moment, imagine an irritable businessperson coming home late at night from work, tired, hungry, and angry. Or imagine a woman who gets cranky for a few days before her period. Both individuals can feel their inner tension mounting by the minute. Although these images of those who benefit from *Nux vomica* are a bit like cartoons, when you consider taking this remedy or giving it to a member of your family, please do remember that people who need *Nux vomica* always possess at least a hint of anger and impatience. Combine these two important features with increased sensitivity to stimuli—sounds, light, and odors—and a *Nux vomica* picture truly emerges. Another highlight of this state of being is the presence of significant digestive problems. Those are its major indicators.

Although *Nux vomica* comes last in our list of seven important homeopathic remedies to keep on hand around your house, it is definitely not the least. In fact, one leading Indian homeopath, N. M. Choudhuri, calls it the "king of all remedies,"[1] as it can implement a cure for more than ten thousand symptoms. There is a term for exceptionally useful remedies like this one (of which there are only a handful)—that term is *polychrest*.[2] According to Dr. Hahnemann:

> *There are a few medicines, the majority of whose symptoms correspond in similarity with the symptoms of the commonest and most frequent of human diseases, and hence very often find an efficacious homoeopathic employment. . . . They may be termed polychrests. . . . To these belong particularly the* Nux vomica *seed . . . it proves the mildest and most efficacious remedy in all the diseases whose symptoms correspond in similarity to the effects* Nux vomica *is capable of producing in the healthy human being, when administered in the small doses.*[3]

In reality, a large proportion of our modern society often finds itself in the *Nux vomica* state—some due to their innate psycho-physiological makeup, others driven to it by constant exposure to stimuli and pressure that make them uncharacteristically irritable. Many of us can get over our symptoms just by resting, eating, and participating in relaxing activities. But some get stuck and need help from *Nux vomica*, the king.

The Origins of *Nux Vomica*

Nux vomica is a medium-sized tree (about thirty-nine to forty-six feet tall) native to India and Sri Lanka. Its fruit, the size of a large apple, is filled with a jellylike pulp and contains five seeds that are shaped like disks. One might compare these seeds to simple buttons, which is where the tree's folk name, Quaker buttons, originated. Because they are hard and therefore difficult to crush, the homeopathic remedy must be prepared starting from an alcohol extract of the "buttons."

As you learned in Chapter 9, *Ignatia* is the sister of *Nux vomica*, as these two remedies are made from botanically related plants. Like *Ignatia*, the chief constituents of *Nux vomica* are strychnine and brucine, which are contained in the tree and its fruit. However, while *Nux vomica* and *Ignatia* are akin and share two active ingredients, albeit in different proportions, their homeopathic actions are quite different.

Prominent American homeopath Robin Murphy has written:

> *The difference in the character of* Ignatia *and* Nux vomica *proves the wisdom of Hahnemann's simple methods of studying medicines. If there was nothing more than the chemistry of the drugs to go by* Ignatia *and* Nux-v *might be used indifferently [for the same symptoms or illnesses]. With the knowledge Hahnemann has given us of their characteristic features they are seldom even thought of in connection with the same case.*[4]

Indeed, as you'll soon see, *Nux vomica* is prescribed for people unlike those who need *Ignatia*.

Homeopathic provings have allowed us to perceive the fine distinctions between the qualities of various medicinal substances. Just to give you an idea of how significant the differences are in this particular case, let's investigate, with the help of a computer. Modern homeopathic software offers many valuable features. These programs enable us to analyze what symptoms are unique to one remedy in comparison with another. Accordingly, *Nux vomica* may cure 11,031 symptoms, and *Ignatia* only 5,988. In comparison with each other, out of their entire cataloged symptoms, almost 70 percent of *Nux vomica*'s and 84 percent of *Ignatia*'s symptoms are particular to that remedy.

So as you can clearly see, although these substances have produced some similar symptoms in provings (and thus could cure them), their dissimilarities are so significant that each remedy made from them corresponds to a distinguishable, well-defined state.

Indian folk medicine has found many applications for nonhomeopathic *Nux vomica*. The bark is ground along with black pepper and then made into a paste that is given orally in a single dose for asthma attacks or labor pains. Interestingly, the same preparation is given three times a day for colds and coughs. The *Nux vomica* seed is an ingredient in Indian folk medicine for dog bites and in ointments and lotions for skin diseases. Leprosy is treated with the ground bark of the *Nux vomica* tree.

Europeans first learned about this plant species from the German botanist Valerio Cordo, who described it in 1561. Initially, products made from the tree were used to kill rodents and small predators. Fascinated by the poisonous power of the seeds, European scientists discovered that plants die after their roots are immersed in *Nux vomica* extract. Subsequent studies showed that in small doses this plant could be helpful for various ailments. Only Hahnemann was able to discover the full range of its medicinal applications.

Symptoms Characteristic of the *Nux Vomica* State

The attributes of the classic type A personality closely match the description of typical symptoms calling for *Nux vomica*. According to Vijay P. Sharma, Ph.D., "There are two cardinal features of type A that we must remember, namely, 'time urgency or time-impatience' and 'free-floating (all pervasive and ever-present) hostility.'"[5] Whereas type B personalities are laid back and easygoing, type A personalities are workaholics, always busy, driven, impatient, and so on. Likewise, someone in a *Nux vomica* state is impatient, angry, ambitious, and confident to the point of being arrogant.

Type A behavior was discovered and researched in the 1950s after two American cardiologists, Meyer Friedman, M.D., and Ray Rosenman, M.D., both noticed that the edges of chairs in their waiting rooms were worn out. They hypothesized that patients at high risk for coronary disease were driven, impatient people who sat on the edges of their seats before appointments. In 1974 they reported their insightful observations in a popular book, *Type A Behavior and Your Heart*.

Elaine Woo, a *New York Times* staff writer, states:

"Type A personality" soon became part of the national vocabulary, shorthand for the sort of driven individual who feels oppressed by time. This is the person who honks and fumes in traffic, barks at sluggish salesclerks, and feels compelled to do several things at once—perhaps shave while paying bills and dialing a phone.[6]

Think about a person who requires *Nux vomica* as somebody who is born oversensitive, who therefore tenses up and strains too much. Any condition that begins with the following unique combination of symptoms can be improved by *Nux vomica*:

❀ Irritability due to an overall sensitivity to stimuli of all kinds
❀ Tendency to be very easily offended
❀ Anger on being contradicted
❀ Impatience
❀ Competitiveness
❀ Being chilly
❀ Frequent digestive, spasmodic problems (for example, constipation with the main characteristic of ineffectual urging, which means passing a stool but feeling that one is not done)
❀ Better: from warmth and in hot and humid weather (true for most symptoms)

While it is important to remember that some people are born to react in a *"Nux vomica* way," there are also some circumstances that may trigger this combination of symptoms, including:

* Prolonged, stressful work
* Working night shifts
* Overindulgence in food and stimulants, such as coffee
* Drug and alcohol abuse

Digestive Problems

Before we delve into all the various remedies for digestive problems, I have an obligation to inform you honestly that our famous gastroenterologist, the king, has a rival. This polychrest, *Arsenicum album* (arsenic trioxide), is such a powerful contender that bestselling author Chris Bohjalian mentions the remedy several times in his novel *The Law of Similars*.[7] *Arsenicum album* is not included in our list of seven main remedies for a simple reason. For acute ailments, perhaps with the exception of flu, colds, and diarrhea, its application is rarely obvious. Nonetheless, this remedy remains important, and you must be able to clearly understand the differences between it and *Nux vomica*.

The need for *Nux vomica* presents itself through symptoms that result from living life on overdrive. People in a *Nux vomica* state become increasingly sensitive and, as a result, irritable and cramped up. People who need *Arsenicum album* have a different set of issues. Usually they are suffering from a loss of structure or support, two things they need in order to feel OK in their lives. As a result, they feel anxious and restless and ultimately become exhausted. Metaphorically speaking, while a "plant" person (*Nux vomica*) is sensitive, a "mineral" person (*Arsenicum*) thrives on structure. People who need *Nux vomica* are angry, whereas *Arsenicum* people are anxious. *Nux vomica* people tend to get constipated. *Arsenicum album* people tend to develop diarrhea.

People who need *Arsenicum album* have other unique characteristics, such as burning pains that get better from warm applications and heat and a constant thirst for small sips of cold water. They also want fresh air. You might find a person who needs *Arsenicum album* bundled up with his head in close proximity to an open window.

Now let's compare *Nux vomica* with other remedies good for digestive problems.

Constipation

Nux vomica is one of the main remedies for constipation, especially spastic constipation.

As this is often a complicated ailment to treat, perceiving a difference among the possible homeopathic remedies that might cure it requires professional training and years of experience. Use *Nux vomica* when you notice some of these characteristic symptoms:

❀ Constipation as a result of a stressful, sedentary, overindulgent lifestyle
❀ Constipation associated with hemorrhoids (also see the section specifically treating this topic)
❀ Frequent desire to pass a stool but with ineffectual urging
❀ Frequent trips to the bathroom, with straining but passing only small quantities
❀ Feeling of unfinished, unsatisfactory stool followed by return trips to the bathroom in an attempt to achieve completion
❀ Constipation that alternates with diarrhea
❀ Irritability, with headaches and upset stomach

I am listing only two other basic remedies here, with obvious, easy-to-appreciate symptoms, as I've seen so many cases in which one of these three remedies made a big difference. Try your best to match *Nux vomica* or one of these alternatives to your condition. Then take three to five pellets of your chosen remedy in 12C potency twice a day for a week or two. If your condition doesn't improve during that time period, seek the guidance of a trained homeopath. Some people may need to repeat their chosen remedy later, after an initial improvement, but this need typically will occur less and less often.

Alumina (aluminum). This remedy is especially good for older people, during pregnancy, and for constipated newborns and bottle-fed infants. Watch for these signs:

❀ No desire to pass a stool (in infants, the desire appears only when there is a large amount of stool; they may experience painful urging)

Table 10.1 Constipation Remedy Comparison Chart

Remedy	Better	Worse	Emotional State
Alumina	No specific modalities	Potatoes	Dull; confused (gets clearer by the end of the day)
Bryonia	Rest	No specific modalities	Irritable
Nux vomica	Warmth; a complete bowel movement	Cold; emotional stress	Irritable; angry

❖ Sensation (in pregnant women) of extreme dryness in the rectum
❖ Need to strain very hard to pass even a soft stool (in some cases, stool has to be removed by hand)
❖ Dry, hard stool that comes out in knots
❖ Cutting pains in the anus while passing a stool, with possible bleeding

The following symptoms don't necessarily have to be present, but if they are there, your remedy for sure should be *Alumina*:

❖ Mental dullness, confusion, and slow response
❖ Cravings for dry foods (e.g., dry rice) and inedible things (e.g., earth, coal, and chalk)
❖ Aversion to potatoes or easily upset stomach from eating potatoes (I know, it sounds strange; nonetheless, it is a valuable symptom)

Physical Problems	Signs Guiding Your Selection	Food Cravings
Vertigo on closing the eyes; dryness of the mouth, rectum, and skin	No urging for stool; constipation during pregnancy with extremely dry rectum; constipation with soft stool	Craving for dry foods (e.g., dry rice); craving for inedible things (earth, coal, chalk); aversion to potatoes
Bitter taste in the mouth; headache that is made much worse by even the slightest movement	No desire to pass a stool; burnt-looking stool	Craving for large amounts of cold liquids
Chill; generally worse in the morning	Strong urges to pass a stool but with very little output; feeling of needing to go again after a bowel movement	Craving for stimulants (coffee, alcohol, and spicy food)

Bryonia alba (white bryony). Like *Alumina*, this remedy is quite helpful for elderly people and pregnant women. It is also useful in treating infants, especially when they're teething. Signs that it is the right remedy to take include:

* ❋ No desire for stool (similar to *Alumina*, yet the other indications are different)
* ❋ Dry stool that looks burnt
* ❋ Irritability (compare with *Nux vomica*)
* ❋ Headache that is made much worse by even the slightest movement
* ❋ Constipation that improves from rest
* ❋ Dry mouth with coated tongue
* ❋ Bad, bitter taste in the mouth
* ❋ Great thirst for large amounts of cold liquids

Diarrhea

Once I consulted a couple that shared the same main complaint: they got diarrhea when traveling to an Asian country. I'd previously seen them both for issues unrelated to digestion. From our earlier meetings, I recalled that the wife was an anxious person and the husband was a high-powered businessman. The original matters had resolved quickly. Easy come, easy go. With an easy case, if the patient returns a year or two later, the homeopath isn't likely to remember what remedy was prescribed without looking it up in his or her notes. A difficult case, however, is a totally different story.

So this couple came in, and I began with the wife. The first comment out of her mouth was that she'd also made appointments with an infectious disease specialist and a holistic doctor known to check for parasites, just to make sure she hadn't contracted an incurable tropical illness. I offered her a glass of cool water and, throughout the interview, she sipped it frequently in small portions. She rearranged all the toys I keep for kids in my office. She complained that her stool was frequent and burning. If you are thinking about the remedy *Arsenicum album* at this point, you are correct. That's what I gave her.

When it was the husband's turn, he came in, and I saw that he was very irritated. He had just had a huge argument in the waiting room with another patient over who got to use the phone first (this happened a few years ago, when people were not as attached to their cell phones as they are now). He needed to make a few important phone calls. After the man calmed down, I gently pushed him into a conversation about competitive sports. It turned out that he played tennis and golf. He readily reported that he needed to win all the time and that if he lost he might lose not only the game but also his temper. His food desires were, as he described them, "very traditional." He drank coffee a few times a day, ate rich, spicy food, and had a few drinks after work. He also complained of waking up in the middle of the night thinking about business matters. Furthermore, his diarrhea was special. He had a lot of cramps and felt that his bowel movements, although liquid, were incomplete and unsatisfactory. I gave the man *Nux vomica*, and he got excellent results.

Diarrhea is one of the few conditions for which the benefits of homeopathy have been repeatedly demonstrated in well-designed clinical studies. Here *Nux vomica*'s rival *Arsenicum* definitely has the upper hand; nonetheless, you would select *Nux vomica* if the following symptoms were exhibited:

❊ Frequent ineffectual urges to have a bowel movement
❊ Cramping with painful diarrhea with an urge again soon after passing a stool (feels incomplete)
❊ Diarrhea after excessive use of alcohol
❊ Diarrhea after experiencing stress related to work
❊ Diarrhea after anger
❊ Better: from warm applications to the abdomen (compare with *Arsenicum*)

Research data show that *Arsenicum* is one of the five most frequently prescribed homeopathic remedies for diarrhea in children.[8] These results hold true for adults, too. Nonetheless, you have many more excellent options from which to choose, at least eight of high merit. Consider this list.

Aloe (aloes).

❊ Sudden urging to pass a stool in the morning, driving a person out of bed (compare with *Sulphur*)
❊ Urge to pass a stool at 5 A.M. (compare with *Sulphur*)
❊ Diarrhea accompanied by a lot of gas and sputtering
❊ Involuntary stool on passing gas
❊ Stool containing jellylike parts of mucus
❊ Better: from lying on the abdomen

Argentum nitricum (silver nitrate).

❊ Diarrhea from anxious anticipation after mental or emotional strain (compare with *Gelsemium*)

Table 10.2 Diarrhea Remedy Comparison Chart

Remedy	Better	Worse	Emotional State	Physical Problems
Aloe	Lying on the abdomen	Overeating; beer; oysters; unripe fruit; 5 to 6 A.M.	No specific symptoms for this condition	Feels warm; dislikes heat
Argentum nitricum	Burping (can be loud)	Drinking; ice-cream; sweets; heat	Warm; extroverted; a bit too open; cocky; lovable; morbidly afraid of heights	Feels hot and bloated
Arsenicum	Heat; warm applications (e.g., warm water bottle) to the abdomen	Cold environment; cold food and drinks; fruit; meat; alcohol; between midnight and 2 A.M.	Anxious; antsy; detail oriented	Always cold; irritating, burning stool; often has significant nausea and vomiting
Chamomilla	Being constantly carried	Heat; being angry; night	Irritable; demanding; capricious; makes everybody around unhappy	Green stool that looks like spinach or chopped grass and has the odor of rotten eggs
China	Warmth; plenty of liquids	Nursing (for babies); significant loss of blood or other bodily fluids; fruit, fish, and milk; every other day, or any periodicity; night	Sensitive to all stimuli; has many thoughts running in the head; may be apathetic	Feels very cold; significant indigestion (feels like food is just lying in the stomach); very weak; pale with large circles under the eyes
Gelsemium	No specific modalities for this problem	Anticipation; thinking about illnesses; walking	Timid; anxious; likes to be alone	Trembling from anxiety; fatigued; sticky sweat all over body

Signs Guiding Your Selection	Food Cravings and Aversions	Remedy to Compare With
Sudden urge for stool in the morning; lots of gas; involuntary stool on passing gas	Craving for juicy things; aversion to meat	*Arsenicum; Podophyllum; Sulphur*
Diarrhea from anxious anticipation (stage fright)	Craving for sweets	*Gelsemium; Sulphur*
Food poisoning; overeating fruit; diarrhea every morning in the elderly; chronic diarrhea in alcoholics	Craving for water in small sips; craving for sour things, whiskey and wine, and fat (also likes warm food)	*Argentum nitricum; Gelsemium; Veratrum album*
Diarrhea in infants and small children; diarrhea during teething and colic	Craving for coffee (in adults)	*Nux vomica; Sulphur*
Diarrhea after prolonged exhausting diseases and after blood loss; hungry without appetite	Craves sour fruit	*Arsenicum; Gelsemium*
Diarrhea from anticipation	No thirst	*Argentum nitricum; Arsenicum*

continued

Table 10.2 Diarrhea Remedy Comparison Chart *(continued)*

Remedy	Better	Worse	Emotional State	Physical Problems
Nux vomica	Warmth; a complete bowel movement	Cold, emotional stress	Irritable; angry	Chilly; generally feels worse in the morning
Podophyllum	Cramps are better from passing stool (temporarily)	Hot weather; eating or drinking; early morning (4 to 5 A.M.)	Not much going on emotionally	Weak; feels like fainting; empty sensation in the stomach after passing a stool
Sulphur	No modalities specific for this condition	Beer; sweets; milk; early morning (5 to 6 A.M.)	Warm and open; can be short tempered but quickly calms down; remains cheerful and in good spirits	Feels hot; stool burns and smells very bad
Veratrum album	Warmth	Extreme heat or cold	Often described as "sullen indifference"; feels wasted	Exhaustion; cold sweat, especially on forehead

❊ Diarrhea accompanied by abdominal rumbling, bloating, and gas (an important point to distinguish from the symptoms of *Gelsemium*)

❊ Feeling of being very warm

❊ Extroverted, cheerful, perhaps too open, and cocky demeanor (compare with the shy, quiet type who benefits from *Gelsemium*)

❊ Morbidly afraid of heights

❊ Better: from burping, which can be pretty loud

❊ Worse: immediately after drinking water and from lying on the left side, sweets (that someone who needs this remedy craves), and heat

Signs Guiding Your Selection	Food Cravings and Aversions	Remedy to Compare With
Strong urges for stool but with very little output; urge to go again soon after a bowel movement	Craving for stimulants (coffee, alcohol, spicy food)	
Severe diarrhea when stool is explosive and soils the entire toilet bowl and even the buttocks	No specific cravings or aversions	*Arsenicum; Sulphur*
Offensive, burning diarrhea	Craving for cold drinks; craving for sweets, carbs, and spicy food; aversion to fish (though there are exceptions to this rule)	*Podophyllum*
Simultaneous diarrhea and projectile vomiting; exhaustion; excessive cold sweat	Craving for ice-cold drinks, as well as for salty and sour food	*Arsenicum*

Arsenicum album (arsenic trioxide). Consider using this remedy first in cases of food poisoning.

* Diarrhea possibly accompanied by nausea and vomiting (compare with *Veratrum album*)
* Chronic diarrhea in alcoholics
* Morning diarrhea in the elderly
* Liquid stool that frequently looks like rice water, is caustic, and burns
* Thirst for small sips of cold water
* Chill, anxiety, and restlessness

* Possibly, fear of dying from diarrhea or some terrible underlying illness
* Better: from warm applications to the abdomen
* Worse: between midnight and 2 A.M.

Chamomilla (German chamomile). This is often appropriate for treating diarrhea in infants and toddlers, especially when symptoms emerge in combination with teething.

* Sensitivity, irritability, and tendency to complain
* Capriciousness (asks for things that are later rejected)
* Desire to be carried all the time
* Green stool with the odor of rotten eggs (compare with *Sulphur*)

China (*Cinchona officinalis*).

* Diarrhea during or after prolonged, exhausting illnesses (for example, AIDS) or following the loss of fluids (such as results from heavy bleeding or prolonged nursing)
* Diarrhea only at night
* Tremendous weakness, sometimes with trembling
* Desire for sour fruit—and diarrhea after eating the fruit
* Pale eyes with dark circles under them

Gelsemium sempervirens (yellow jasmine).

* Diarrhea from anticipation or fright (compare with *Argentum nitricum*)
* Painless diarrhea
* Possibly, diarrhea accompanied by frequent urination
* Weak and shy demeanor

Podophyllum (mayapple). This remedy is frequently indicated for the treatment of diarrhea. Famous homeopath Roger Morrison writes, "The efficacy of *Podophyllum* in acute diarrhea is so marked that our thoughts turn automatically to this remedy in such a condition, and must be forced by symptoms to look elsewhere."[9]

To make the differentiation between this remedy and *Arsenicum* crystal clear, the rule of thumb is always to consider this remedy first in cases of severe diarrhea and to think of *Arsenicum* first in cases of food poisoning. Other remedies are only prescribed when you can see their most prominent symptoms or if you cannot find clear symptoms of either *Podophyllum* or *Arsenicum*.

People who need *Podophyllum* do not show a lot of anxiety. They are simply tired and exhausted from having diarrhea. Look also for:

* Abundant, watery, noisy, explosive diarrhea
* Much gas
* Stool that soils the entire toilet bowl and the buttocks
* Feeling of wanting to faint and being very weak
* Gurgling before passing stool
* Empty sensation after passing stool
* Stool often with terrible offensive odor
* Possibly, a headache from diarrhea
* Possible rectal prolapse from diarrhea
* Worse: from heat, from hot weather, in the morning around 4 to 5 A.M. (compare with *Arsenicum*), and from any movement

Sulphur (brimstone).

* Urgent stool that wakes the person around 5 or 6 A.M. (compare with *Podophyllum*)
* Painful stool with soreness and burning of anus
* Stool with a horrific odor, frequently described as similar to the odor of rotten eggs (the entire household knows that the person is having a bowel movement, and the smell is so foul that people won't want to enter the bathroom for a long time)
* Feeling of being hot during diarrhea (for *Arsenicum*, there is a feeling of being chilly)
* Frequently, hunger and cheerfulness
* Falling asleep immediately after the fit of diarrhea
* Thirst for large amounts of cold drinks

Veratrum album (white hellebore).

* Severe exhaustion, which accompanies *Arsenicum*-like symptoms but without any anxiety (this is the key to this remedy)
* Diarrhea accompanied by cold sweats, especially on the forehead
* Diarrhea simultaneously with profuse forceful vomiting (compare with *Arsenicum*)
* Exhaustion, weakness, and maybe even fainting after passing a stool
* Sometimes a peculiar sensation of feeling coldness in the abdomen
* Worse: from heat (compare with *Arsenicum*)

Hemorrhoids

Treatment of this problem can be complicated, particularly in cases where hemorrhoids are merely a segment of a complex set of health issues. That said, even the external use of homeopathic preparations can provide significant relief. In fact, most hemorrhoid sufferers I've seen in my practice swear by homeopathic suppositories and ointments. You can easily locate these types of products in health food stores that carry homeopathic preparations. All of the major homeopathic companies make them.

Please be mindful of these two important points before you start on a course of self-treatment for hemorrhoids:

* Consult with your primary physician to find out as much as you can about the underlying cause of your hemorrhoids.
* If you are under the care of a homeopath for any reason, please do not self-prescribe for hemorrhoids, especially if your main complaint has been improving. Give the remedy you are taking, or have taken, a chance to produce a cure.

Nux vomica is appropriate for extremely sensitive, painful hemorrhoids that appear in combination with stubborn constipation. It is appropriate when you see several items from the following constellation of symptoms:

* Hemorrhoids after overindulgence (too much coffee or too much alcohol)
* Hemorrhoids after abuse of laxatives
* Irritability, being on edge
* Better: after stool
* Worse: from alcohol, stimulants, and movement

Now let's talk about several additional remedies. These are the remedies most frequently needed, and they are easy to distinguish. If, in your case or that of a family member, you find it too difficult to choose the correct remedy from the short list that follows, or if you would like to enhance the action of your current homeopathic or allopathic treatment for this condition, remember what you learned a few paragraphs ago about using homeopathic ointments or suppositories to gain temporary relief.

Aesculus (horse chestnut). This is the core remedy in most homeopathic ointments and suppositories for hemorrhoids. It is also correct to take it in tablet form when:

* Painful hemorrhoids are associated with lower back pain
* There's a feeling that the rectum is filled with splinters
* There's a sensation that the stool is rough or coarse
* Hemorrhoids occur during pregnancy
* Better: in a kneeling position and from taking a warm bath
* Worse: from standing

Aloe (aloes).

* Large hemorrhoids that protrude like a bunch of grapes
* Loose or uncomfortably open, dragging sensation in the rectum
* Occasionally, involuntary stool, especially on passing gas
* Better: from cold bathing (compare with *Aesculus* and *Sulphur*)
* Worse: from sitting and during menses

Table 10.3 Hemorrhoids Remedy Comparison Chart

Remedy	Better	Worse	Emotional State	Physical Problems
Aesculus	Kneeling; warm bath	Standing	Irritable	Lower back weakness and pain; feeling as if rectum is filled with splinters; hemorrhoidal pains that last hours after passing a stool
Aloe	Cold bath	Sitting; beer	No specific symptoms for this condition	Loose feeling in the rectum, as if the sphincter is wide open; burning from passing gas; involuntary stool
Hamamelis	No specific modalities	Warmth and heat	No specific symptoms for this condition	Raw, sore anus
Ignatia	Walking or sitting (paradoxical modalities)	Emotional upset; passing a stool; lying down at night (paradoxical modalities)	Easily hurt; hysterical; touchy and defensive	Paradoxical reactions: feels better in the rain but worse from lying down, and so on; back spasms from grief, lump in the throat (could be in the rectum)
Nux vomica	Bowel movement	Alcohol; abuse of laxatives; any type of overindulgence; motion	Irritable; angry	Chilly; generally worse in the morning
Paeonia	Lying down after passing a stool, with legs and buttocks held spread apart	Slightest touch, even gently wiping after a bowel movement	Can be nervous and anxious with bad dreams and even nightmares	May have ulcers on the skin
Ratanhia	Warm bath; lying down; walking slowly	Passing a stool	Obsessive thoughts with compulsive rituals	Tendency to have fissures in various locations of the body

Signs Guiding Your Selection	Food Cravings and Aversions	Remedy to Compare With
Painful hemorrhoids plus lower back pain; hemorrhoids during pregnancy	No specific cravings or aversions for this problem	*Nux vomica; Paeonia; Ratanhia*
Large hemorrhoids protruding like a bunch of grapes	Craving for juicy things; aversion to meat	*Hamamelis; Sulphur*
Large, blue hemorrhoids that bleed easily	No specific data	*Aloe*
Hemorrhoids and fissures with extremely painful rectal spasms, as if a knife were stuck in the rectum; pain worse from emotional problems and better from walking and sitting	Craving for cheese; aversion to fruit	*Nux vomica; Ratanhia*
Painful hemorrhoids and fissures in combination with persistent constipation	Craving for stimulants (coffee, alcohol, and spicy food)	*Ignatia*
Extremely painful hemorrhoids after passing a stool (better from lying down with legs and buttocks held spread apart)	No specific data	*Aesculus; Ignatia; Nux vomica; Ratanhia*
Pain that gives the sensation of having broken glass in the rectum; combination of hemorrhoids and obsessive behavior	No specific data	*Ignatia; Nux vomica; Paeonia*

continued

Table 10.3 Hemorrhoids Remedy Comparison Chart *(continued)*

Remedy	Better	Worse	Emotional State	Physical Problems
Sulphur	Cold bath	Standing; beer; night in bed	Warm and open; can be short tempered but quickly calms down; remains cheerful and in good spirits	Feels hot; burning stool that smells very bad; itchy rectum, which gets worse from scratching

Hamamelis virginiana (witch hazel). Together with *Aesculus*, this remedy is frequently a component of hemorrhoid suppositories and ointments. Look for:

❖ Weakness of all veins and varicose veins
❖ Large blue, protruding hemorrhoids that bleed when passing a stool

Ignatia amara (St. Ignatius's bean).

❖ Hemorrhoids with extremely painful rectal spasms that appear or get worse after emotional distress
❖ Pain that feels like a metal rod or a knife was stuck in the rectum
❖ Better: from walking or sitting (here we go again—a paradoxical symptom)
❖ Worse: from lying down at night, from emotional trouble, and at the end of passing a stool (and another paradoxical symptom; compare with *Nux vomica* and *Ratanhia*)

Paeonia (peony).

❖ Tremendous pain after passing a stool (compare with *Ratanhia*)
❖ Better: from lying down with legs and buttocks spread (if clear, this symptom alone dictates the use of this remedy; if this symptom is absent, think about *Ratanhia* instead)

Signs Guiding Your Selection	Food Cravings and Aversions	Remedy to Compare With
Large hemorrhoids with terrible itching	Craving for cold drinks; craving for sweets, carbs, and spicy food; aversion to fish (though there are exceptions to this rule)	*Aesculus*

* Worse: from even the slightest touch while wiping after a bowel movement

Ratanhia (mapato).

* Incredible, excruciating pain after passing a stool (pain may last for minutes or even hours)
* Frequently, a sensation of having broken glass in the rectum
* Better: from walking slowly, lying down, and taking a warm bath
* Worse: after passing a stool and from hard stool

Sulphur (brimstone).

* Hemorrhoids with overpowering, irresistible itching
* Usually, personable, extroverted, friendly, and emotionally warm demeanor but with poor grooming
* Warm-blooded
* Extremely malodorous stool
* Better: from taking a cold bath
* Worse: at night (especially the itching) and from drinking beer or standing

Nausea and Vomiting

This section will cover a handful of remedies that resolve most cases of uncomplicated nausea and vomiting. Everyone knows how common both these problems are. Many people suffer from seasickness or carsickness. Pregnant women often complain about morning sickness. Other people get nauseous from overeating, and still others from food poisoning. Sadly, nausea is also frequently a complication of chemotherapy for cancer.

Please remember that persistent feelings of nausea and/or frequent vomiting need to be investigated by a physician. This caution is especially applicable to newborns, babies, and pregnant women. There are numerous easily treatable and potentially life-threatening causes of nausea and vomiting, such as alcohol abuse, drug abuse, PMS, pregnancy, food intolerance, peptic ulcer, vertigo, headache, hepatitis, and cancer. Don't hesitate long in seeking professional help if these problems are persistent, or if the initial nausea or vomiting is severe, or even if they were relieved by homeopathy. You should always consult with a trained homeopath when confronting serious and chronic problems or if your initial attempts to find a correct remedy on your own have failed.

As you may be aware, many people have used raw slices of ginger, boiled ginger water, and tea to decrease and even eliminate their feelings of nausea. Some also find it helpful to drink diluted apple cider vinegar. To prepare, combine one or two teaspoons of apple cider vinegar with a glass of water (cold or, if you like it better, at room temperature). You may also add honey to taste. Drink small sips of this beverage throughout the day.

The best tactic for overcoming nausea and vomiting with homeopathic remedies is to take three pellets of 30C concentration of a remedy after each episode of vomiting. If the remedy works, the episodes should become less frequent and disappear in the course of a day or two. For cases of nausea that arise during chemotherapy, take your chosen remedy once daily for the duration of chemotherapy and/or nausea.

Nux vomica may be appropriate for symptoms of nausea and vomiting that occur as a result of alcohol and drug abuse, for nausea during constipation, and for nausea accompanied by unsuccessful and painful attempts to vomit, by cramps, and/or by painful episodes of vomiting. Look also for characteristic signs, such as:

❀ Anger and irritability
❀ Hypersensitivity to stimuli—sounds, light, odors, touch, and so on
❀ Better: from lying down, warm drinks, and food
❀ Worse: in the morning and from eating, alcohol, being angry, and cold drinks

If symptoms pertaining to *Nux vomica* are not present in your situation, try one of the following homeopathic remedies instead.

Aethusa cynapium (fool's parsley).

❀ Vomiting in nursing babies
❀ Vomiting of milk in curds
❀ Sleepiness after vomiting, followed by hunger, eating, and then more vomiting
❀ Worse: from milk

Antimonium crudum (antimony sulphide).

❀ Thick white-coated tongue
❀ No symptoms typical of other remedies
❀ Worse: from drinking, becoming warm, rich foods, and wheat-containing foods

Arsenicum album (arsenic trioxide).

❀ Food poisoning
❀ Burning pains in the stomach or along the esophagus that accompany vomiting
❀ Anxiety, fearfulness, and restlessness during vomiting or with nausea
❀ Chill
❀ Vomiting accompanied by diarrhea (compare with *Veratrum album*)
❀ Thirst for sips of cold drinks, followed by vomiting immediately after drinking them (compare with *Phosphorus*)

Table 10.4 Nausea and Vomiting Remedy Comparison Chart

Remedy	Better	Worse	Emotional State	Physical Problems
Aethusa	Company; open air	Heat; summer; evening	Irritable; tearfulness	Gets colicky, irritable, and exhausted and then goes to sleep
Antimonium crudum	Open air; rest	Drinking; becoming warm; carbs	Difficult to please; irritable; contradictive; children don't like to be touched or looked at; adults are less obvious about these things	Thick white-coated tongue; dry lips
Arsenicum	Warm drinks	Cold drinks; the smell and even the thought of food; midnight	Anxious; fearful (afraid of having a serious illness)	Cold, burning pains in the stomach with every fit of vomiting; vomiting may be accompanied with diarrhea
Bryonia	Lying absolutely still; being left alone; cold drinks	Even the slightest movement	Irritable	Dry, dirty-looking tongue
Cocculus	Lying on the side; warm room	Movement or even watching objects move; open, cold air	Full of concerns; may be irritable	Vertigo; metallic taste
Colchicum	Leaning forward	Odor, sight, or even thought of food; pregnancy	No relevant data	Extremely weak; feels cold inside or has burning and distension of the stomach; pupils may be of different size (confirms the remedy but is not always present)
Ipecacuanha	Nothing makes nausea better except for this remedy	Periodically, lying down	May be irritable	Clean, red tongue despite nausea

Signs Guiding Your Selection	Food Cravings and Aversions	Remedy to Compare With
Vomiting curds of milk soon after nursing	Little baby—eats only mother's milk or formula	
Nausea with indigestion; tongue covered with thick white coating	Craving for sour food, including pickles	*Bryonia; Ipecacuanha; Nux vomica*
Food poisoning; vomiting of cold drinks immediately after swallowing	Craving for sips of cold water	*Colchicum; Phosphorus; Veratrum*
Nausea provoked by the slightest movement	Craving for large amounts of cold water	*Veratrum*
Motion sickness	Craving for cold drinks, especially beer; complete aversion to any type of food	*Kreosotum; Tabacum*
Nausea and vomiting of pregnancy	Craving for many types of food (but nauseous at the sight of them); craving for alcohol	*Arsenicum; Kreosotum; Sepia*
Severe nausea with no relief even from vomiting	No specific data	*Antimonium*

continued

Table 10.4 Nausea and Vomiting Remedy Comparison Chart *(continued)*

Remedy	Better	Worse	Emotional State	Physical Problems
Kreosotum	Warmth; warm food	Time before menses and during pregnancy; cold food	Capricious	Vomits several hours after eating; has bitter taste upon swallowing water
Nux vomica	Lying down; warm drinks and food	Being angry; cold drinks and food; morning	Irritable; over-sensitive; angry	Chilly; constipated
Phosphorus	Lying on the right side; sleep	Warm drinks and food; general anesthesia	Cheerful	Remains in good shape despite nausea and vomiting
Sanguinaria	Vomiting; acidic food; sleep; darkness	Sweets; motion	No specific data	Various right-sided problems (e.g., migraine)
Sepia	Eating; strenuous exercise	Time before breakfast	Cries easily; may be depressed; decreased energy from 3 to 5 P.M.	Exhausted; most complaints are better from exercise
Tabacum	Open, fresh air (like on the deck of a moving ship or by the open window of a moving car)	Extreme heat or cold	May be irritable	Extremely pale coloring (described by some as green)
Veratrum album	Night, after sleep	Walking; warmth	In a stupor from exhaustion	Exhausted with cold sweat on the forehead and cold breath

Signs Guiding Your Selection	Food Cravings and Aversions	Remedy to Compare With
Vomiting several hours after eating; nausea before menses and during pregnancy	No specific data	*Colchicum; Sepia*
Nausea and vomiting from drug and alcohol abuse and from constipation; cramps in the stomach during vomiting	Craving for stimulants (alcohol and rich and spicy food)	*Arsenicum*
Vomiting of cold drinks after they become warm in the stomach	Craving for cold water and salty things	*Arsenicum; Nux vomica; Veratrum*
Nausea and all other complaints much better after vomiting; nausea with salivation	Unquenchable thirst; aversion to butter	
Morning sickness of pregnancy; nausea after chemotherapy	Sour, sweet and sour food	*Colchicum; Kreosotum; Ipecacuanha*
Severe nausea (usually seasickness or car sickness) better from fresh air	No specific data (though some people crave tobacco)	*Cocculus*
Projectile vomiting simultaneously with diarrhea	Craving for ice-cold water and salty things (even raw salt)	*Arsenicum; Phosphorus*

❖ Better: from warm liquids
❖ Worse: after midnight, from cold drinks, and from the smell or even the thought of food (if this symptom is very strong, compare with *Colchicum*)

Bryonia alba (white bryony).

❖ Vomiting provoked by even the slightest movement
❖ Better: from lying still and cold drinks (compare with *Arsenicum album*)
❖ Worse: from movement, trying to sit up in bed, raising the head, and coughing

Cocculus indicus (Indian cockle).

❖ Motion sickness (always compare with *Tabacum*—*Cocculus* is worse from open air, *Tabacum* is better from open air)
❖ Nausea when watching moving objects (nausea in people who need this remedy comes from the brain, not from the stomach)
❖ Nausea in people exhausted by night vigilance (for example, sitting up with a severely ill friend or relative)
❖ Extreme weakness, even to the point of trembling
❖ No tolerance for the smell of food or even for thinking of food (compare with *Arsenicum* and *Colchicum*)
❖ Better: from lying down on a side or being in a warm room (compare with *Tabacum*)
❖ Worse: from movement

Colchicum (meadow saffron).

❖ Nausea from the odor, the sight, or even the thought of food
❖ Feeling of faintness from food odors (often experienced by pregnant women with this particular symptom)
❖ Extreme sensitivity to rudeness (also frequently observed in pregnant women)

Ipecacuanha (ipecac root).

❄ Awful nausea not relieved at all by vomiting (compare with *Sanguinaria*)
❄ Clean, red tongue despite digestive problems and nausea (compare with *Antimonium*)
❄ In my experience, often helpful for nausea during or after chemotherapy
❄ Except for this remedy, nothing makes this nausea feel better

Kreosotum (beechwood creosote).

❄ Nausea and vomiting up food undigested long after eating
❄ Very valuable in cases of vomiting during PMS or pregnancy
❄ Drinking water produces bitter taste
❄ Worse: before menses and during pregnancy and from cold food and meat

Phosphorus (phosphorus).

❄ Cold drinks vomited after they become warm in the stomach (not immediately, like in *Arsenicum*)
❄ Craving for large amounts of cold drinks (compare with *Arsenicum*'s small sips)
❄ Often remains cheerful and functions OK despite vomiting (compare with *Arsenicum* and *Veratrum*)
❄ Better: temporarily from cold drinks, after sleep, and from lying on the right side
❄ Worse: from warm drinks and food (compare with *Nux vomica*) and after general anesthesia (a remedy of choice for this problem)

Sanguinaria canadensis (bloodroot).

❄ Symptoms that are greatly relieved by vomiting
❄ Right-sided migraines
❄ Bitter, caustic vomitus

Sepia (cuttlefish ink). One of the most important remedies for morning sickness in pregnancy, *Sepia* is also an important potential remedy for nausea after chemotherapy (compare with *Ipecacuanha*).
Characteristic symptoms include:

* Possibly, motion sickness
* In cases of morning sickness, no tolerance for husband's smell
* Weakness and indifference to people she usually loves
* Possibly, postnasal discharge
* Better: from eating, especially sour food, and from strenuous exercise
* Worse: before breakfast, during sex, or even from the thought of sex

Tabacum (tobacco).

* Very important for cases of seasickness (amazingly, in days of yore, most of the pirates and old skippers smoked a pipe)
* Deathly, severe nausea
* Extremely pale coloring, described by some as green
* Light-headedness with a cold sweat and a feeling that one is about to faint
* Better: from open air (compare with *Cocculus*)

Veratrum album (white hellebore).

* Projectile vomiting that is simultaneous with diarrhea
* Complete exhaustion with a cold sweat on the forehead and sometimes cold breath
* Frequently, craving for ice-cold drinks and/or ice, as well as salt
* Worse: after sleep (compare with *Phosphorus*)

Hay Fever and Other Acute Allergies

In addition to being a gastroenterologist, *Nux vomica* has another terrific specialty. It's an allergist. As I mentioned before, polychrests like *Nux vomica* can be used to treat many different conditions with thousands of symptoms. Long live the king!

Seasonal allergies (aka hay fever) are enormously common, affecting at least 35.9 million people in the United States alone. In fact, approximately 16.7 million office visits to U.S. health care providers each year are attributed to allergic rhinitis. The American Academy of Allergy, Asthma and Immunology offers these additional statistics:[10]

❋ Estimates from a skin test survey suggest that allergies affect as many as 40 to 50 million people in the United States.

❋ Allergic diseases affect more than 20 percent of the population in the United States.

❋ Allergic diseases are the sixth leading cause of chronic disease in the United States.

Interestingly, homeopaths pioneered both the research and the treatment of allergies. In 1871 British homeopath C. H. Blackely suggested that seasonal sneezing and nasal discharge were the results of exposure to pollen. Later prominent American homeopath James Tyler Kent defined the practical principles of treating allergies with homeopathy. If someone develops an acute reaction (such as a running nose or itching, watery eyes) to pollen or another allergen during the allergy season, this reaction is addressed first. After all, there is no need for anyone to suffer discomfort. Then during the symptom-free season, a homeopath aims to find a so-called constitutional remedy that solves the problem on every level of a person's being. It can take a while for the full effects of a remedy like this to be felt. But in the end, many other complaints usually drop away along with the symptoms of allergy.

Today conventional allergists use a desensitization process that resembles the homeopathic practice of using like to cure like. They give their patients a bit of the allergen to stimulate a reaction that the body overcomes, thus making the body stronger. However, their injections do not feature homeopathically prepared solutions, nor do

Table 10.5 Hay Fever and Other Acute Allergies Remedy Comparison Chart

Remedy	Better	Worse	Emotional State
Allium	Open, cold air	Warm, stuffy room; late afternoon and evening	Has difficulty thinking
Apis	Cold applications	Heat	Irritable; needs to move
Arsenicum	Warm applications; warm room; warm drinks	Cold	Anxious; fearful of serious, incurable illness
Euphrasia	Lying down in bed at night; coffee	Morning	No data
Nux vomica	Waking up in the morning; open air; eating meals	Warm room	Irritable; oversensitive to all stimuli
Sabadilla	Heat; being in a warm room; warm drinks	Cold temperature; open air	Anxious; timid
Urtica	No modalities	Water; cool moist air; touch	No data

allergists take an individual's characteristic symptoms into consideration. It's a little-known fact that a homeopath, Grant L. Selfridge, M.D., was the first president of the organization that is now the American Academy of Allergy, Asthma and Immunology.

Physical Problems	Signs Guiding Your Selection	Remedy to Compare With
Stuffy nose; heaviness at the base of the nose	Bland discharge from the eyes and irritating discharge from the nose	*Euphrasia; Arsenicum*
Significant redness, swelling, stinging (like from a bee sting), and pain	Allergic reactions to bee stings; allergic reactions with swelling and redness; skin hot to the touch; much improvement from ice-cold applications	*Urtica urens*
Mainly right-sided problems; irritating watery dripping from an obstructed nose	Irritating discharge from the nose; improvement from warmth	*Allium; Euphrasia; Sabadilla*
Center of the problems is in the eyes	Irritated, burning, itching eyes; abundant tears; bland nasal discharge	*Allium*
Cold; prone to spasms	Stuffed, dry nose at night; sneezing and discharge from the nose in the morning	*Allium; Sabadilla*
No thirst; desire for hot food	Fits of sneezing that may sound like an automatic weapon; itchiness inside the nose and/or of the palate	*Arsenicum; Nux vomica*
Tendency to have hives and blotches	Allergic reactions to shellfish	*Apis*

Here is an interesting educational case from my practice. As often happens, a family member who was cured from a long-standing migraine headache asked me whether I could help a man with severe seasonal allergies. Because it was allergy season, I saw a window of opportunity to come in with a homeopathic remedy at a time when all his shields were down—to address his raw, painful symptoms. The man came in the next week and presented, as his main complaint, frequent sneezing. Sometimes he sneezed more than ten times in a row right on waking up. The remedy listed in this chapter for this symptom is *Sabadilla*. Everyone who knows homeopathy will tell you that with this symptom alone, the likelihood of the patient needing *Sabadilla* is high.

The next step in my thinking process (and it should also be the next step in yours) was to see what other characteristic mental symptoms, generalities, and modalities I could find. If there were no mental symptoms and the patient had told me that the only other symptoms he had were sneezing (mostly in the morning) and having his palate itch, *Sabadilla* would move right to the top of the list of possible remedies and win. But the man also complained of waking up every night around 3 A.M., thinking about his new job.

Furthermore, he said that his nose felt stuffed all the time. He was pretty intense, on edge, irritable, and easily offended. He said he needed to eat a lot of dark chocolate every day (in my head this is a stimulant similar to coffee). He also said that even though he knew that spices made his sneezing worse, he ate Indian food almost every day. He complained of constipation and told me that after he sneezed, he felt unsatisfied, like he needed to sneeze more to finish the job. Using your imagination, can you easily picture that this feeling of incompleteness after a sneeze is not so different from the feeling of incompleteness after a bowel movement? In the big picture, that is.

Guess what? I gave him *Nux vomica*. It was a total success. As you can see very clearly from this case, I just went with the flow of his symptoms. I did not pull anything out of him with forceps. It was a clean, simple case with an easy (for you and me) solution. You'll probably see more cases of *Sabadilla*, *Euphrasia*, and *Allium cepa* (all described shortly) for hay fever, but remember that *Nux vomica* is always standing by, just in case.

This book offers you a few solutions for simple acute problems, such as might arise during allergy season or after eating an unfamiliar food. Beside the homeopathic remedies, I also recommend trying a combination of one or more of the following natural solutions, as these are often very effective.

❋ **Extract of eyebright and stinging nettles.** (Herb Pharm makes a product called Eyebright/Nettle Compound; other herbal companies have similar products.) Take ten drops three times a day. As you read forward, you'll notice that homeopathic preparations of both of these herbs are listed for the treatment of allergies. Don't worry about taking the herbs and remedies simultaneously. Nonhomeopathic preparations of herbs do not counteract the effects of homeopathy.

❋ **Bioflavonoids.** I recommend taking between 3,000 and 4,000 milligrams a day (each tablet or capsule contains 1,000 milligrams).

❋ **Eliminate wheat and/or dairy from your diet.** For some people, eliminating wheat and dairy does miracles. For others, it has no impact on their allergies.

Nux vomica is the correct remedy for your own or your family's allergies if you see the following characteristic symptoms:

❋ Sneezing and discharge from the nose upon rising from bed in the morning
❋ Dry, sore, stuffed nose at night while in bed
❋ Irritability
❋ Better: from being in a warm room (in some cases, the nose completely clears up) and from warm drinks
❋ Worse: on waking up in the morning, after meals, and from open air

If those symptoms are not present, consider one of the following remedies instead.

Allium cepa (red onion).

❋ Always compare with *Euphrasia*
❋ Caustic discharge from the nose that irritates the nose and the upper lip (opposite of *Euphrasia*)

❋ Bland discharge from the eyes (opposite of *Euphrasia*)
❋ Discharge from the nose and eyes in copious amounts
❋ Eventually, completely obstructed nose
❋ Frequently, heaviness in the middle of the forehead and/or a headache that gets better when the nose drains freely
❋ Origin of headache frequently on the left side
❋ Better: from open, cold air
❋ Worse: in the late afternoon and evening and from being in a warm room

Apis mellifica (honeybee). More times than not, this is the right remedy for allergic reactions to bee stings. Be prepared to give it on the way to the emergency room. Also use for any severe allergic reaction that involves the combination of symptoms that follow.

❋ Very significant swelling of the eyes (sometimes eyes are literally bloodshot from swelling)
❋ Heat and burning sensation of the face and the eyes
❋ Craving for cold applications with much improvement by them
❋ The person who needs *Apis* may become unusually irritable and snappy

Arsenicum album (arsenic trioxide).

❋ Irritating watery discharge from the nose
❋ Dripping from the nose, which is completely obstructed
❋ Burning (eyes, nose, throat) that is better from hot drinks or hot applications
❋ Mainly affects right side
❋ Better: from being in a warm room, warm drinks, and warm applications (compare with *Allium cepa*)
❋ Worse: from anything cold

Euphrasia officinalis (eyebright).

❋ Always compare with *Allium cepa*
❋ Irritated, burning, itching eyes

* Abundant, irritating tears and bland nasal discharge (exactly opposite of *Allium cepa*)
* Better: upon lying down in bed at night
* Worse: in the morning and from warm wind

Sabadilla (cevadilla seed).

* Remarkable fits of sneezing (some people sound like an automatic weapon)
* Sneezing fits that always provoke tears
* Constant itchiness inside the nose and/or of the palate
* Better: from heat, being in a warm room, and warm drinks
* Worse: from open, cold air

Urtica urens (stinging nettle). This remedy is specifically used for allergic reactions to shellfish. Look for:

* Itching hives with a prickling, burning sensation
* Hives that look like red, raised blotches with white centers

A Few More Conditions That May Require *Nux Vomica*

As you may recall from previous chapters, *Nux vomica* is often indicated for headaches, especially those that frequently come as a result of tension at work or working too much. The person who needs *Nux vomica* is very irritable during the headache. I can still remember the headaches I used to get from moonlighting in the emergency room after a full day of work and almost no sleep. *Nux vomica* 30C helped me quite a bit. It also helps people who lose sleep as a result of working hard and playing hard.

Obviously, if you had spent the day on the trading floor of the Stock Exchange and then went out with your friends and had a few drinks, your sleep would not be the greatest. The same idea applies to coming home from a large wedding party. An acute hangover may respond very nicely to *Nux vomica*.

Just remember that *Nux vomica*, or any other remedy, won't help a chronic alcoholic recover unless he or she wants to. One needs to see exactly what remedy is indicated, and that is a job for an experienced homeopath working in accord with other drug or alcohol treatment professionals. *Nux vomica* is the king of all remedies, not just the king of recovering alcoholics.

And let's not forget about man's best friend: PMS. Even a PMS queen might meet her match in *Nux vomica*. Of course, PMS is terribly uncomfortable for the women who endure it month after month, and for this reason, I really shouldn't joke about it. But there's good news. Homeopathy can help. Because there are many things about PMS that can complicate the selection process, sufferers really need to work with a trained homeopath who can help them make the right choice.

Another important idea for you to appreciate is that homeopathy helps to cure various digestive problems. I certainly have seen many cases when homeopathic remedies resulted in significant relief for people with irritable bowel syndrome and even Crohn's disease. Treatment of these illnesses has to be provided by a trained homeopath. A famous label "indigestion" covers so many various potentially serious chronic problems that advising you on self-treatment would be unwise.

PART

3

HELPFUL HINTS
AND EASY
SOLUTIONS

 **11**

Remedies for Common Ailments

When you're prepared, you're more confident. When you have a strategy, you're more comfortable.

— FRED COUPLES

M Y IDEA HERE is to offer you a homeopathic cheat sheet for acute conditions so you'll be able to orient yourself quickly when handling different types of situations, spanning from anger and kidney stones to sore throats and varicose veins. You may be able to get away just with using the information presented in this chapter, or you may need to return to a chapter that corresponds to one of the book's seven central remedies. Then, with the advantage of having a fairly good idea in mind of your remedy of choice, you'll swiftly be able to confirm its key symptoms or find out that you need a different remedy.

Note: some conditions listed in the following pages aren't included in the chapters on the seven remedies. In such cases, you'll be offered one or two choices of commonly indicated remedies for these ailments. When appropriate, I'll also talk about herbs and supplements that can be used to enhance the action of the homeopathy.

Remember, if you can clearly see the main characteristics of *any* of the remedies described in the earlier chapters, give that remedy *regardless* of the diagnosis and short recommendations you find in this chapter.

Allergies (Acute)

Homeopathy

Take three 30C pellets of either of the following remedies every fifteen minutes three times in a row. Stop if there is a 50 percent improvement, even after the first dose. Stop if there is no improvement at all or if you feel worse. In cases of severe allergic reactions, take the remedy on your way to the ER.

Apis mellifica. This is for allergic reactions to bee stings and for any allergic reaction with significant swelling, redness, and local pain. Often the victim also feels irritable.

Urtica urens. This is for allergic reactions to shellfish.

Herbal Preparations

A good addition to homeopathy is extract of eyebright and stinging nettles. (Herb Pharm makes a product called Eyebright/Nettle Compound; other herbal companies have similar products.) Take ten drops three times a day.

Anger

Chamomilla. This is for babies and toddlers, especially during teething, as well as for women during a difficult, painful delivery. Give three 30C pellets dry or in water each time there is an angry outburst. Stop if better. Also stop and consult a homeopath if there was no effect at all after the first dose.

Nux vomica. This is for intense, overworked, stressed-out, driven, career-oriented people, as well as for angry people who work many hours in a row and are on edge, their nerves raw. Take three 30C pellets. Repeat the dose three times every fifteen minutes if there was an initial response. Stop when 50 percent better. See a homeopath if there was no effect after three doses.

Anxiety

Aconitum napellus. This is for severe restless panic with a fear of death.

Argentum nitricum. Restless, wants company, talks a lot.

Gelsemium sempervirens. Feels paralyzed from anxiety, wants to be left alone. Quiet, shy.

Bites

Ledum palustre. Consider this remedy first for any bite. This is for insect (for example, wasp, tick, or any large insect), animal, and human bites. Take three 30C pellets three times every fifteen minutes.

Carbolicum acidum. This is for severe allergic reactions to bee stings, insect bites, and animal bites; it's also useful for anaphylaxis.

The victim has a dusky red face. The skin around the mouth and nose is pale. The victim also reports a choking feeling and frequently becomes lethargic but, even so, may paradoxically develop an acute awareness of odors. In cases of allergic reactions, a person develops hives over the entire body.

Call 911 immediately or go to the ER if you see these symptoms develop. You can always give a remedy on your way to the ER. Give three 30C pellets every ten to fifteen minutes until improvement or the arrival of an ambulance.

Oxalicum acidum. This remedy works well for bites from poisonous snakes or spiders if the affected part becomes numb and cold to the touch. The victim also reports violent pains and begins to tremble. It's imperative to rush the victim to the nearest hospital! Give three 30C pellets every ten minutes on your way to the ER.

Bladder Infection

Recurrent infections should be treated by a homeopath (which should give you good results). You have a very small window of opportunity. Try your remedy of choice for a few hours. If you don't get at least 50 percent better, start conventional treatment right away. I always advise taking the best remedy you can pick and going to see a conventional physician. If the remedy kicks in and you feel better before filling a conventional prescription, great. If not, well, you have a prescription in hand ready to go to the pharmacy.

Take three 30C pellets of any remedy in the following list three times at intervals of thirty minutes. After initial improvement, you can continue taking the remedy every two hours until the problem is gone. If there is no effect at all after the initial three doses (meaning within two to three hours), start conventional treatment.

Cantharis. This is the most common remedy for acute urinary infections. Severe burning pain with urination is the main problem.

Nux vomica. The person has a feeling of fullness and constant urging, but urine is passed in small amounts with a sensation of incompleteness and a need to urinate again.

Petroselinum sativum (parsley root). This is frequently indicated in children. Severe itching deep in the urethra is the key. Sufferers get sudden urges that cause them to jump and have pain if they do not urinate immediately.

Pulsatilla nigricans. The sufferer experiences paroxysmal pain and very strong urges and cannot hold the urine. Pain gets progressively worse with attempts to hold back the urine.

Sarsaparilla (sarsaparilla). The sufferer passes large amounts of urine with severe pain at the end of urination.

Bruises

Arnica montana. Take three 200C pellets immediately after injury. To prevent bruising and other complications after plastic surgery, simply use SinEcch (from Alpine Pharmaceuticals). It is *Arnica* conveniently prepackaged in capsules and labeled with easy-to-follow instructions. You can find it on the Internet and in some health food stores. Please remember that taking *Arnica* too frequently may cause increased bruising due to the proving effect.

I also recommend using a combination of *Arnica* and *Hamamelis* ointments (gel, cream, or lotion) to be applied externally twice a day. *Warning:* never apply these ointments on cuts (surgical or otherwise).

Ledum palustre. This is for bruises at the site of a bite or a puncture wound or for large bruises after fractures. The area feels cold to the touch. Bruises get better from applications of ice. Take three 30C pellets once a day until you see 50 percent improvement.

Sulphuricum acidum. This remedy is used in cases where large bruises don't go away after using *Arnica*. Pain is relieved by warm applications. Take three 30C pellets once a day until you see 50 percent improvement.

Burns (Minor)

Please remember to seek professional help (go to the ER) in every single case of a serious burn or when burns seem to be minor but are extremely painful and begin to blister. You can take a remedy on your way to the ER.

At home, start by placing your extremity under running cold water for about fifteen minutes. Never place ice directly on your skin!

For minor burns only, aloe vera ointments (cream, lotions) are effective. Do not apply ointment in cases of blisters or broken skin.

Use remedies in 30C concentration. Take three pellets every fifteen to twenty minutes until you see marked improvement. Stop after three initial doses if you don't feel better.

Apis mellifica. Skin is red, swollen, and painful. Pain is relieved only by ice-cold applications. (*Cantharis* has the same characteristics in cases of serious second-degree and third-degree burns.)

Urtica urens. This is for scalding from boiling or hot water. There is an itching sensation that accompanies the usual burning pain.

Chicken Pox

In most countries, this illness has practically been eliminated due to vaccination. But if somebody contracts it, homeopathy is helpful. Be aware, however, that in the beginning of the illness you might need the usual remedies for colds and flu.

Antimonium crudum. Take three 30C pellets three times (morning, noon, and night) on the first day.

Colds

Homeopathy

Oscillococcinum. This is a proprietary single remedy produced by Boiron. It should be used at the first sign of a cold or flu. Easy-to-follow instructions are printed on the package.

For a more sophisticated, individualized approach, refer back to Chapter 4.

Herbs and Supplements

You may use extracts of echinacea and astragalus. Take ten drops of each three times a day for up to seven days.

Vitamin C. This is for adults without any chronic health problems. Take 500 milligrams in a chewable tablet every hour until you reach a daily dose of 3,000 milligrams (usually six tablets altogether).

Colic

Chamomilla. This is the most commonly prescribed remedy for irritable children who want to be carried at all times. Give three 30C pellets once.

If there is no effect, refer back to Chapter 7 to select a more appropriate remedy.

Constipation

Nux vomica. This is for frequent, ineffective urges and the feeling of incompleteness after a bowel movement. Take three 12C pellets every day for a week.

If there is no effect, refer back to Chapter 10. And if you cannot find your symptoms in that chapter, consult a homeopath.

Cough

Homeopathy

Refer back to Chapter 4 if you are showing symptoms of cough and flu.

Herbs and Supplements

Take extract of echinacea for a dry cough. And take extract of echinacea along with extract of mullein for a wet cough. Take ten drops of each three times a day. Also take 2,000 to 3,000 milligrams a day of chewable vitamin C. Usually this combination takes care of mild cases of uncomplicated coughing. For an irritating dry cough, also drink mint tea or suck on lozenges containing mint (peppermint).

Croup

Croup has the potential to be a dangerous condition. So give the best remedy you know on your way to the ER. Better safe than sorry.

For the two following remedies, it is appropriate to give a child three 30C pellets every fifteen to twenty minutes. Stop if there is a significant improvement, and then give an additional dose each time the child begins to feel worse. Discontinue if there is no effect after three repetitions. For more details, refer back to Chapter 4.

Aconitum napellus. This is for the very beginning of illness. The child is morbidly scared.

Spongia tosta. This is good for later in the course of the illness or at the onset if there was never an *Aconitum* stage. The child improves from warm drinks.

Detoxification from Drugs or Alcohol

Consider the following two remedies. For either, it is appropriate to take three 30C pellets three times a day.

Nux vomica. This remedy is the absolute king of detox. The person who needs it is usually extremely sensitive to all sensory stimulation and is irritable and angry.

Ignatia amara. Consider this remedy if there is a prominent hysterical, emotional component to the detoxification process with a lot of sighing and crying.

Diarrhea

Homeopathy

For more details, refer back to Chapter 10. If the remedy you choose is correct, episodes will become less and less frequent. Take three 30C pellets after each episode of diarrhea.

Arsenicum album. This is for food poisoning and is the first consideration in any case of diarrhea.

Podophyllum. This is for explosive, noisy diarrhea that soils the toilet bowl and frequently also the buttocks. The sufferer feels very weak after passing each stool.

Veratrum album. This is for profuse, odorless stool. Simultaneously the person has forceful vomiting and becomes weak with cold sweat.

Additional Measures

It is all right to take over-the-counter medications that contain bismuth, such as Pepto-Bismol, as these don't interfere with homeopathy. And be sure to drink a lot of liquids containing sodium and potassium (for example, Gatorade). In addition, stop eating sweets, carbohydrates, dairy, and spicy food. If you cannot live on small quantities of food, consider the BRAT diet (banana, white rice, grated apple, and plain toast). I prefer a combination of rice and tea (black or green) without sugar.

Ear Infections (Acute)

Warning: always go see a doctor if there is discharge from the ear.

Homeopathy

See a clear description of major remedies in Chapter 6.

Herbs

Put a few drops of lukewarm mullein oil in the ear to stop the pain. Do not infuse the ear in this way if there is discharge.

Fainting

Carbo vegetabilis. Take three 30C pellets every fifteen minutes until better, a maximum of three times. Stop taking it if there is no effect after these three doses.

Fatigue (Acute)

For more details, refer back to Chapter 8. Take three 30C pellets of one of the two following remedies three times a day for up to a week.

Stop if there is significant improvement. Also discontinue if there is no improvement at all in three days.

China. Use after the significant loss of fluid (including prolonged bleeding).

Gelsemium sempervirens. This is frequently indicated after mononucleosis. You should always think about this remedy in cases of fatigue that accompanies neurological problems.

Fear of Dentists, Doctors, and Surgery

Aconitum napellus. This is for people who are morbidly afraid with a fear of death. It is also for people, including children, who fear going to a doctor or a dentist even in an emergency. Take three 30C pellets the morning of the scheduled visit and immediately beforehand.

Fever

See the "Colds" section in this chapter as well as Chapter 4 for details.

Flu

See the "Colds" section in this chapter as well as Chapter 4 for details.

Food Poisoning

Arsenicum album. Take three 30C pellets every fifteen minutes three to five times. Stop if there is a significant improvement even after the first dose. Also discontinue if there is no improvement after the third dose.

Fractures

Aconitum napellus. If there is the initial shock with severe fear, take three 200C or 30C pellets a few times at fifteen- to twenty-minute intervals. Stop if there is significant improvement. Also discontinue if there is no change after the first two doses.

Arnica montana. Give three 200C pellets within the first hours after the fracture. Repeat if necessary. The remedy reduces bruising, swelling, and pain.

Bryonia alba. The sufferer cannot even sneeze, as any movement causes severe, sharp pain. Give three 30C pellets every thirty minutes. Stop if there is significant improvement. Also discontinue if there is no change after the second dose.

Hypericum perforatum. This is for crushed fingertips and is also a specific remedy for a compound fracture, an injury "that occurs when there is a break in the skin around a broken bone."[1] Give three 30C pellets three times every fifteen minutes, and then give three 30C pellets once a day for three days.

Ruta graveolens. This is for injuries to the shin, kneecap, and elbow, places where the bone is close to the surface. It is also for chronic pain after a fracture is healed but gets worse in cold, damp weather. Take three 12C pellets every day for twenty days.

Symphytum officinale. This helps bone to grow quickly. Give only after the fracture has been set! Take three 12C pellets once a day for twenty days.

Frostbite

Of course, frostbite is a rare occurrence in most of the world, except possibly among skiers. But in some colder places (like Alaska, Siberia, or regions high in the mountains) it happens relatively frequently.

Secale cornutum. Take three 30C pellets every fifteen minutes. Stop after three to five doses or earlier if there is significant improvement. Discontinue if there is no effect after three doses. Repeat as needed if symptoms that initially improved come back.

Gas/Bloating

Frequently a chronic problem, this condition requires a visit to a homeopath. Following are two remedies that can be helpful in acute situations. Also don't forget about activated charcoal, as it can provide temporary relief from bloating and doesn't interfere with homeopathy.

Take three 30C pellets of either of the following remedies once and then wait for about an hour. If there is no effect at all, the remedy you selected was wrong. If the effect is incomplete, you may repeat the dose as needed. Discontinue after three doses, or stop earlier if your symptoms improve significantly.

Nux moschata. This is for terrible distension immediately after eating, accompanied by constipation and foul-smelling gas. Though the mouth is dry, the sufferer is not thirsty. The sufferer craves spicy food, becomes drowsy, and may even faint.

Nux vomica. This is for distention from overindulgence in food, drinks, and drugs, as well as for distention after significant stress. The sufferer usually feels worse a few hours after eating.

Grief

Ignatia amara. This is the absolute leader in the area of grief. Take three 200C pellets immediately after a breakup or getting bad news. If you are the bearer of bad news, try to give the remedy fifteen to thirty minutes before telling the person about the situation. On the first day, it can be repeated two more times. Then use as needed.

For more details about other options, refer back to Chapter 9.

Growing Pains

Calcarea phosphorica. Give three 200C pellets once. Then in two weeks, start taking five 6X tablets of *Calcarea phosphorica* cell salts twice a day.[2] Use them for two to three months. This remedy helps to form strong bones and teeth and reduces growing pains.

Hay Fever

For a clear description of a few helpful remedies, see the "Allergies" section in this chapter, and refer back to Chapter 10.

Headache (Acute)

Iris versicolor. This is frequently indicated for classical migraine headaches that begin with visual aura and end with vomiting, as well as for blurry vision and sometimes even blindness during a headache. Take three 30C pellets every fifteen minutes a maximum of three times. Stop if there is a significant improvement sooner.

For more details, refer back to Chapter 8.

Head Injury

Arnica montana. Take three 200C or 30C pellets three times on the day of the injury. Please remember that head injuries with even a short loss of consciousness require a detailed medical workup. Take yourself (or the victim) to the doctor or ER even if you feel good. One of the main symptoms of *Arnica* is to believe you don't need help, remember?

Hemorrhoids

Aesculus (horse chestnut). Take three 30C pellets a day for a few days. Stop the moment there is significant improvement. Also discontinue if there is no marked improvement after three days. Combine with homeopathic hemorrhoid suppositories.

Nux vomica. This is for painful hemorrhoids in combination with constipation in overindulgent, irritable people. Follow the regimen described for *Aesculus*.

For more details, refer back to Chapter 10. Remember that chronic hemorrhoids require a visit to a homeopath.

Herpes Zoster (Shingles)

Homeopathy

For chronic, recurrent cases, see a homeopath. It is appropriate with the following three remedies to take three 30C pellets twice a day for three days. Discontinue if there is no effect or if you feel worse.

Apis mellifica. This is for lesions on the face, especially on the left side.

Arsenicum album. This is for pain that is burning and is relieved by warm applications.

Ranunculus bulbosus. This is the remedy of choice for shingles on the left side of the chest.

Supplements

Lysine. Take 500 milligrams twice a day.

Vitamin C. Take 500 milligrams twice a day.

Hives (Acute)

Chronic hives require a visit to a homeopath.

Urtica urens. Take three 30C pellets three times a day. Stop if the condition improves earlier. Discontinue if there is no effect after three doses.

Indigestion

Take three 30C pellets of either of the following remedies three times a day for one day. Stop if the condition improves sooner. Also discontinue if there is no effect after three doses.

Arsenicum album. This is for indigestion from eating too much fruit. The person is frequently anxious.

Nux vomica. This is for indigestion from overeating, along with irritability and constricting pains.

Injuries

Arnica montana. This remedy should always be considered first. Refer back to Chapter 5 for detailed information on the treatment of injuries.

Insect Bites and Stings

Give three 30C pellets of either of the following remedies three times every fifteen minutes.

Apis mellifica. This is for stings by bees and other small insects. The site of the bite is hot to the touch, red, and swollen. The person is frequently (but not always) irritable.

Ledum palustre. This is for stings and bites by large insects (wasps, for example). The site of the bite is cold to the touch and has a bluish tinge. Paradoxically, the cold-to-the-touch lesion improves from exposure to extreme cold.

Insomnia (Temporary)

Coffea cruda. Take three 30C pellets once. If the remedy does not work or stops working in a while, see a homeopath.

Kidney Stones (Acute Pain While Passing the Stone)

In this section, we are talking only about acute pain that occurs while passing a kidney stone.

Warning: a kidney stone must pass relatively quickly. If the stone does not pass in twenty-four hours, you must see a urologist. Long-standing obstruction can cause permanent damage to your kidney. It is better to involve a urologist rather early. You don't have to wait for a day. Do what seems to be reasonably safe. I would go sooner myself.

Take three 30C pellets of either of the following remedies three times a day. Continue for two to three days. Homeopathy also can help resolve the general issue of producing stones, but that requires consultation with a professional homeopath.

Belladonna. This is for terrible sudden pain, usually on the right side. The face is flushed and red. Hands and feet are cold. The sufferer is restless and much worse from the slightest jarring.

Berberis vulgaris. This is for sharp, shooting, or constricting pain that radiates in different directions. More frequently, the left kidney is involved.

Mastitis (Breast Infection)

In my experience, homeopathy helps this problem very well. But frequently it requires the involvement of a homeopath. If you have no access to a homeopath and have tried a remedy without any effect, go and see a conventional physician.

Phytolacca decandra. Very frequently (but far from always) this remedy solves the problem. Take three 30C pellets three times a day for a few days. Stop after significant improvement or if the problem gets worse. Also discontinue if there is no effect in three days.

Mental Fatigue/Exhaustion

Picricum acidum. This is for exhaustion after long studies, such as cramming for exams, or after other prolonged intellectual strain. Take three 30C pellets once a day for three days.

Milk Intolerance in Babies

Benign in the majority of cases, this symptom could be a part of a more serious problem, such as the result of birth injury or digestive problems. If the vomiting persists for more than a few days despite treatment, make sure to consult with a pediatrician. Projectile vomiting in a baby warrants an immediate visit to a doctor. Better safe than sorry.

Aethusa cynapium. The baby vomits milk in curds soon after the end of feeding. To prepare, place three 30C pellets in a teaspoon with a small amount of springwater, and then crush them with another teaspoon placed on top. Give the mixture to the baby after each episode of vomiting. If the remedy is effective, you will see vomiting happen less and less frequently. Stop if there is no improvement in two to three days.

Motion Sickness (Seasickness)

There are two predominant remedies for this condition: *Cocculus* and *Tabacum*. Give three 30C pellets of either remedy, for a maximum of three times, at fifteen- to twenty-minute intervals. In cases of seasickness, you'll see people who need *Cocculus* down below and people who need *Tabacum* up on deck.

Cocculus indicus. The sufferer feels worse from open air and better from lying on a side in a warm room.

Tabacum. The sufferer turns pale (almost green) and feels much better from fresh air.

Nausea and Vomiting

Refer back to Chapter 10 for clear information.

Nightmares

Nightmares respond well to homeopathy, although you may need to get a homeopath involved. I've seen numerous cases where parents gave their children *Stramonium* with great success and all I had to do was approve their decision. Unfortunately, this remedy is becoming more and more commonly needed.

Stramonium. This is for severe nightmares. A combination of nightmares, fear of the dark, fear of dogs, stammering, and clingy behavior points to *Stramonium* with a high level of probability. A combination of nightmares with even one of these other symptoms could be a good enough sign it is needed. The child also may be violent.

Give three 30C pellets and wait. If the condition improves in a few weeks and then comes back in a month or more, repeat *Stramo-*

nium by giving three 200C pellets. You still may need to repeat the dose every few months, though less and less frequently.

Pinkeye (Conjunctivitis)

This condition responds well to homeopathy. See a homeopath if the choice of the remedy is difficult or unsuccessful.

Homeopathy

Give three 30C pellets three times a day. The correct remedy improves the condition in twenty-four hours.

Pulsatilla nigricans. This is the most frequently indicated remedy, especially in babies and older children. The eye is red, and there is thick yellow greenish discharge from the inner part of the eye. In cases of allergic inflammation of the eye, there is a tremendous itching.

Argentum metallicum. The person wakes up and cannot open the eyes because they are glued shut by an enormous amount of pus. This is most frequently indicated in adults.

Herbs

Wash the eyes (first the healthy eye and then the sick one) three to four times a day with either eyebright tea or eyebright extract that's been diluted 1:15 in distilled water.

Warning: ensure that the liquid is at room temperature. If there is a lot of pus, adding calendula extract in the same proportion is a good idea.

Poison Ivy/Poison Oak

Poison Ivy Pills. This product manufactured by Washington Homeopathic Products contains *Rhus toxicodendron* 4X. Pills come with clear instructions for use. The company claims an 80 percent success rate and also advises customers to use the product for prevention. Most of my patients find it effective if started at the first sign of trouble.

Sinusitis (Acute)

Treatment of sinusitis, both acute and chronic, is a definite forte of homeopathy. My personal experience is a good testimony to that. Best results are achieved when sinusitis is treated by an experienced homeopath. On the other hand, if you catch the first episode of sinusitis with the correct remedy, the problem may be solved for a long time.

Constitutional treatment may take longer than one appointment (similarly to any other type of illness). In cases of acute problems, just try your best. Remember, if you fail, antibiotics are always an option. After a course of antibiotics is completed, see a homeopath for constitutional treatment.

Homeopathy

Take three 30C pellets of any of the following remedies three times a day for three days. Stop any time there is significant improvement. Discontinue after three days.

Hydrastis canadensis. This is indicated when nasal discharge is green, copious, and thick. There is significant postnasal drip, frequently along with a sore throat. People who need it usually are constipated.

Kali bichromicum. This remedy is indicated significantly more often than *Hydrastis.* Nasal discharge is gluey, sticky, and thick greenish yellow and comes out in long strings. The voice sounds nasal due to complete nasal obstruction that often is present. There is a significant heaviness, fullness, and burning pain at the root of the nose. If there is any problem with the stools, it's usually diarrhea. (The *Hydrastis canadensis* picture has constipation.)

Mercurius vivus. This is also frequently indicated, but unlike cases of *Kali* and *Hydrastis*, the green nasal discharge flows easily and doesn't create long strings of mucus. It is most often indicated in cases of frontal sinusitis. Pains are worse at night, breath has an offensive odor, and there are tooth imprints on a coated, dirty-looking tongue as well as drooling. You can easily appreciate this symptom if you see wet spots on the pillow in the morning.

Herbs, Supplements, and Other Supportive Measures

Frequently, these steps alone resolve most of the mild sinusitis cases.

❋ Avoid dairy and wheat. This step alone makes a significant difference for a number of patients. Many patients also find eating pickled ginger and wasabi mustard helpful. Obviously, they put the mustard on something (for example, vegetable sushi).

❋ Learn to use a neti pot, which solves many sinus-related problems. A neti pot is a small container with a spout used to wash the sinus cavities.

❋ Use a humidifier at night.

❋ Boil some unpeeled potatoes and inhale the steam for five minutes twice a day with your head over the pot and covered with a towel.

❋ Drink hot tea with lemon, honey, and one-eighth of a teaspoon of cayenne pepper.

❋ Use echinacea and goldenseal extract (sold in the same container by many companies). Take ten drops three times a day for up to seven days.

Sore Throat

See a clear, detailed description of what to do in Chapter 6.

Spinal Injury

Take three 30C pellets three times a day for two to three days. In cases of severe trauma, take three 200C pellets three times every fifteen minutes on your way to the ER.

Arnica montana. This is for acute strains of the back as a result of heavy lifting or whiplash. Someone in an *Arnica* state usually minimizes the seriousness of the injury. Bruised, sore feeling. No urine after spinal injury.

Hypericum perforatum. This is the most important remedy for spinal injuries, especially when pain shoots up the spine or there is an injury to the tailbone. This is also the remedy of choice for severe headaches and pains after a spinal tap.

Rhus toxicodendron. This is for sprains of the lower back and neck. The sufferer feels worse at the onset of motion but gets much better as slow motion continues. Sitting for a long time makes things worse; motion and heat make things better. The person usually has difficulties staying still.

Sprains and Strains

Take three 30C pellets of any of the following remedies three times a day for two to three days. Discontinue after three days.

Arnica montana. This is for a sore, bruised feeling. It is frequently indicated for people who have exercised too much and too long after an extended break from exercise or for people who have just started exercising. The person won't let anyone touch the injured site and might say, "I'm OK—it'll go away soon." (Of course, don't hesitate to use the remedy even if this last symptom is absent.)

Bryonia alba. Think about this remedy first for ankle sprains and strains. The sufferer cannot tolerate even the slightest motion and wants to stay still.

Rhus toxicodendron. This is the most frequently indicated remedy for sprains and strains. The person cannot stay still and is annoyed by stiffness (the main complaint) and pain. The condition gets worse on the first motion but improves as the motion continues and is much better from heat and hot showers. You can also apply *Rhus toxico-dendron* ointment twice a day.

Stage Fright

Look in the "Anxiety" section of this chapter for *Argentum nitricum* and *Gelsemium*. Also refer back to Chapter 8.

Sunstroke

For details, refer back to Chapter 6.

Glonoine. This is the remedy of choice for most cases. Give three 30C pellets one time. Move the victim into the shade, apply cold, and provide liquids. In severe cases, call 911 right away.

Surgery

Refer back to Chapter 5 for a detailed explanation of helpful remedies.

Teething

Chamomilla. This is the remedy of choice. For more details, refer back to Chapter 7.

Varicose Veins

Varicose veins can be complicated by inflammation (phlebitis) and/or clotting (thrombosis). In these cases, seek immediate professional help. In many uncomplicated cases, a homeopath can provide effective help. One remedy is most frequently indicated.

Hamamelis virginiana. This works for many uncomplicated cases of varicose and spider veins. Take three 12C pellets every day for four weeks, and then stop. Repeat after a few weeks' break, if still needed. Also apply *Hamamelis* ointment twice a day, simultaneously with the oral administration.

Wrist Conditions

Ruta graveolens. This is a specific remedy for wrist and tendon problems. For severe conditions and acute trauma, take three 30C pellets three times a day for three days. For long-standing problems, take three 12C pellets once a day every day for a month.

Your Emergency/Travel Homeopathic Kit

It's a good idea to put together a kit of remedies that will help you stay well in many critical situations you could face on the road or at home. I suggest the following remedies:

Aconitum napellus 200C
Apis mellifica 30C
Arnica montana 200C
Arnica montana ointment (or gel)
Arsenicum album 200C
Belladonna 200C
Chamomilla 30C

Cocculus indicus 30C
Gelsemium sempervirens 30C
Ferrum phosphoricum 200C
Ignatia amara 200C
Mercurius vivus 30C
Nux vomica 30C
Pulsatilla nigricans 30C
Rhus toxicodendron 30C
Tabacum 30C

Notes

Chapter 1

1. Vithoulkas, G. *The Science of Homeopathy.* New York: Grove Press, 1980.
2. Kipling, R. *The Jungle Book.* Chapter 1: "Mowgli's Brothers." Website: readbookonline.net.
3. Henry, O. "Hygeia at the Solito." Website: readbookonline.net.

Chapter 2

1. Website: thefreedictionary.com.
2. Studies reliably distinguishing the placebo effect from homeopathy include the following:

    Merrell, W. C., and E. Shalts. "Homeopathy." *Medical Clinics of North America* 86, no. 1 (2002): 47–62.

    Frei, H., R. Everts, K. Von Ammon, F. Kaufmann, D. Walther, S. F. Hsu-Schmitz, M. Collenberg, K. Fuhrer, R. Hassink, M. Steinlin, and A. Thurneysen. "Homeopathic Treatment of Children with Attention Deficit Hyperactivity Disorder: A Randomised, Double Blind, Placebo Controlled Crossover Trial." *European Journal of Pediatrics,* July 27, 2005.

    Frass, M., M. Linkesch, S. Banyai, G. Resch, C. Dielacher, T. Lobl, C. Endler, M. Haidvogl, I. Muchitsch, and E. Schuster. "Adjunctive Homeopathic Treatment in Patients with Severe Sepsis: A Randomized, Double-Blind, Placebo-Controlled Trial in an Intensive Care Unit." *Homeopathy* 94, no. 2 (April 2005): 75–80.

Kim, L. S., J. E. Riedlinger, C. M. Baldwin, L. Hilli, S. V. Khalsa, S. A. Messer, and R. F. Waters. "Treatment of Seasonal Allergic Rhinitis Using Homeopathic Preparation of Common Allergens in the Southwest Region of the US: A Randomized, Controlled Clinical Trial." *Annals of Pharmacotherapy* 39, no. 4 (April 2005): 617–624.

Bell, I. R., D. A. Lewis, II, S. E. Lewis, G. E. Schwartz, A. J. Brooks, A. Scott, and C. M. Baldwin. "EEG Alpha Sensitization in Individualized Homeopathic Treatment of Fibromyalgia." *International Journal of Neuroscience* 114, no. 9 (September 2004): 1195–1220.

Spence, D. S., E. A. Thompson, and S. J. Barron. "Homeopathic Treatment for Chronic Disease: A Six-Year University Hospital Outpatient Observational Study." *Journal of Alternative and Complementary Medicine*, 11, no. 5 (2005): 793–798.

Witt, C. M., R. Luedtke, R. Baur, and S. N. Willich. "Homeopathic Medical Practice: Long-term Results of a Cohort Study with 3,981 Patients." *BMC Public Health*, 35, no. 1 (2005): 115.

3. According to Avogadro's number, a formula used by chemists to calculate the number of molecules in a given amount of any chemical substance, the original substance in a homeopathic remedy disappears at the potency 12C (dilution 10^{-24}).

Avogadro's number (6.023×10^{-23}) is the number of molecules contained in one mole of a substance. One molecule of a remedy substance in a mole is approximately equivalent to 24X (12C) dilution level. In other words, mathematical calculations show that not one molecule of the original substance can be found in a homeopathic remedy at the 24X (12C) dilution level. This explanation is taken from *Yasgur's Homeopathic Dictionary and Holistic Health Reference* by J. Yasgur. Greenville, PA: Vann Hoy, 1998, 25.

4. Davenas, E., F. Beauvais, J. Amara, M. Oberbaum, B. Robinzon, A. Miadonna, A. Tedeschi, B. Pomeranz, P. Fortner, P. Belon, J. Sainte-Laudy, B. Poitevin, and J. Benveniste. "Human Basophil Degranulation Triggered by Very Dilute Antiserum Against IgE." *Nature* 333, no. 6176 (June 30, 1988): 816–818.

5. Belon, P., J. Cumps, M. Ennis, P. F. Mannaioni, M. Roberfroid, J. Sainte-Laudy, and F. A. Wiegant. "Histamine Dilutions Modulate Basophil Activation." *Inflammation Research* 53, no. 5 (April 2004): 181–188.

If you are interested in looking further into this issue, a good website to start reading is digibio.com (Dr. Benveniste's website).

A good book on homeopathic research is *Homeopathy: A Frontier in Medical Science* by P. Bellavite and A. Signorini. Berkeley, CA: North Atlantic Books, 1995.

6. Chakraborti, D., S. C. Mukherjee, K. C. Saha, U. K. Chowdhury, M. M. Rahman, and M. K. Sengupta. "Arsenic Toxicity from Homeopathic Treatment." *Journal of Toxicology: Clinical Toxicology* 41, no. 7 (2003): 963–967.

7. If you want to learn and understand more about these issues, read "Homeopathic Pharmacy," a chapter by M. Quinn in *Classical Homeopathy*, M. Carlston, editor. New York: Churchill Livingstone, 2003, 149–157.

8. Montoya-Cabrera, M. A., S. Rubio-Rodriguez, E. Velazquez-Gonzalez, and S. Avila Montoya. "Intoxicacion mercurial causada por un medicamento homeopatico" [Mercury poisoning caused by a homeopathic drug]. *Gaceta Medica de Mexico* 127, no. 3 (May–June 1991): 267–270.

9. Datta, S., P. Mallick, and A. R. Bukhsh. "Efficacy of a Potentized Homoeopathic Drug (*Arsenicum Album*-30) in Reducing Genotoxic Effects Produced by Arsenic

Trioxide in Mice: Comparative Studies of Pre-, Post- and Combined Pre- and Post-Oral Administration and Comparative Efficacy of Two Microdoses." *Complementary Therapies in Medicine* 7, no. 2 (1999): 62–75.

Mitra, K., S. N. Kundu, and A. R. Khuda Bukhsh. "Efficacy of a Potentized Homoeopathic Drug (*Arsenicum Album*-30) in Reducing Toxic Effects Produced by Arsenic Trioxide in Mice: II. On Alterations in Body Weight, Tissue Weight and Total Protein." *Complementary Therapies in Medicine* 7, no. 1 (1999): 24–34.

Chapter 4

1. The discovery of Oscillococcinum is interesting. A French physician, Joseph Roy, M.D., introduced it in the 1930s. He thought he'd discovered oscillating bacteria in the blood of patients who had the flu and many other illnesses, including cancer. He called this phenomenon *oscillococcus* (meaning "oscillating round bacteria" in Latin). To date, we don't know what Roy saw under his microscope. Certainly it wasn't a flu virus (you cannot see viruses under a regular optical microscope), nor was it any bacteria we know.

   For his homeopathic preparation, Roy decided to use a particular type of duck that's used in France to prepare delicious duck breast. That's why the remedy is designated with the Latin name *Anas barbariae hepatis et cordis extractum*, meaning an autolysate of Barbary duck liver and heart. Interestingly, it has been shown that fowl is a major reservoir of human influenza viruses. Certainly, this remedy is not the first example, and not the last example, of a medication being introduced on the basis of a wrong theory—and then proven to be effective. Think about the situation with the avian flu today. At this point there is no evidence that Oscillococcinum is effective for this particular type of the flu, but it is certainly worth consideration. (Edward Shalts, M.D., D.Ht., *American Institute of Homeopathy Handbook for Parents*. San Francisco, CA: Jossey-Bass, 2005.)

   The British Journal of Clinical Pharmacology published a large-scale double blind, placebo controlled trial in which 487 patients were recruited by 149 general practitioners (mostly non-homoeopaths) in the Rhone-Alpes region of France during the January–February 1987 influenza epidemic. According to this report, 17 percent of the active treatment group fully recovered, compared to 10 percent of the placebo group. This difference is statistically significant ($p = 0.03$, X2 test).

   Further analysis showed that the effect of Oscillococcinum peaked at thirty-six hours, when 40 percent of recoveries were attributable to the treatment. It was most effective in younger patients (68 percent of recoveries within forty-eight hours in the under-thirties were due to treatment), and when the illness was relatively mild (52 percent of the recoveries from illnesses classified as mild or moderate were due to treatment). Patients on active treatment used significantly less other treatment for pain and fever (50 vs. 41 percent). They also judged the active treatment more efficacious than placebo (61 vs. 49 percent).

2. For more details on research, visit the Homeopathic Educational Services website: homeopathic.com/Merchant2/merchant.mvc?Screen=PROD&Store_Code=HES&Product_Code=QB-INF5.

Chapter 5

1. Hahnemann, S. *Materia Medica Pura*. [Original edition 1830.] New Delhi, India: B. Jain Publishers, 1996, volume 1: 89.

2. *Hildegard's Healing Plants: From Her Medieval Classic Physica.* Boston, MA: Beacon Press, 2002.
3. A modality is a condition that makes the ill person, or a particular symptom, better or worse. It is a circumstance giving rise to an increase or a decrease of a symptom. For instance, the patient is worse (<) from wet weather, after midnight, and from cold drinks. Or the patient is better (>) from heat, from elevating the head, and from warm or hot drinks. Source is *Yasgur's Homeopathic Dictionary* by J. Yasgur. Greenville, PA: Van Hoy Publishers, 1998, 155.
4. Morrison, R., with N. Herrick. "The Bali Tragedy—Homeopaths on Hand to Help." *Homeopathy Today*, December 2002.

Chapter 7

1. Website: holistic-online.com/herbal-med/_herbs/h44.htm.
2. Tyler, V. E. *The New Honest Herbal*, third edition. New York: Pharmaceutical Products Press, 1993, 84.
3. Tyler, M. L. *Homoeopathic Drug Pictures.* New Delhi, India: B. Jain Publishers, 1998, 236.
4. Choudhuri, N. M. *A Study on Materia Medica.* New Delhi, India: B. Jain Publishers, 2003, 270.
5. Rothenberg, A. "Natural Remedies for Colic." *Homeopathy Today*, March 2004.

Chapter 8

1. Felter, H. W., and J. U. Lloyd. *King's American Dispensatory*, 1898.
2. Ibid.
3. Grant, E. C. "Food Allergies and Migraine." *Lancet* i (1979): 966–969.

   Monro, J., J. Brostoff, C. Carini, and K. Zilkha. "Food Allergy in Migraine." *Lancet* ii (1980): 1–4.

   Egger, J., C. M. Carter, and J. Wilson, et al. "Is Migraine Food Allergy? A Double-Blind Controlled Trial of Oligoantigenic Diet Treatment." *Lancet* ii (1983): 865–869.
4. Volger, B. K., M. H. Pittler, and E. Ernst. "Feverfew as a Preventive Treatment for Migraine: A Systematic Review." *Cephalagia* 18 (1998): 704–708.
5. Murphy, J. J., S. Hepinstall, and J. R. A. Mitchell. "Randomized Double-Blind Placebo Controlled Trial of Feverfew in Migraine Prevention." *Lancet* ii (1988): 189–192.

   Johnson, E. S., N. P. Kadam, D. M. Hylands, and P. J. Hylands. "Efficacy of Feverfew as Prophylactic Treatment of Migraine." *British Medical Journal* 291 (1985): 569–573.
6. Developed originally by William Sutherland, craniosacral therapy is "a manual therapeutic procedure for remedying distortions in the structure and function of the brain and spinal cord, the bones of the skull, the sacrum and interconnected membranes." Website: tlccenter.com/glossary.ivnu.

Chapter 9

1. Choudhuri, N. M. *A Study on Materia Medica.* New Delhi, India: B. Jain Publishers, 2001, 501.
2. Website: medical-dictionary.thefreedictionary.com/hysteria.

3. Hoover, T. A. "Opening the Home Medicine Chest—This Too Shall Pass . . . Homeopathic Help for Grief." *Homeopathy Today*, February 2001.
4. You can see a photograph of Jack Lawyer and Seri the elephant in *Homeopathy Today*, October 2005, 23.
5. Website: wrongdiagnosis.com/i/insomnia/stats.htm.

Chapter 10

1. Choudhuri, N. M. *A Study on Materia Medica*. New Delhi, India: B. Jain Publishers, 2003, 733.
2. A polychrest is a homeopathic remedy that, because of its ability to heal many different ailments, is commonly used to treat many people with various ailments. Remedies that have many widespread uses and cover a wide variety of mental, emotional, and physical problems are called polychrests. These remedies have very prominent characteristics. When you can see characteristics of a polychrest in your sick child, give it *regardless* of what specific ailment your child has.
3. Hahnemann, S. *Materia Medica Pura*. [Original edition 1830.] New Delhi, India: B. Jain Publishers, 1993, 223.
4. Murphy, R. *Homeopathic Remedy Guide*. Blacksburg, VA: Hahnemann Academy of North America, 2000, 1249.
5. Sharma, V. P. "Characteristics of 'Type A' Personality." Website: mindpub.com/art207.htm.
6. Woo, E. "Meyer Friedman: Doctor Identified 'Type A' Behavior." *Los Angeles Times*, May 6, 2001, B12.
7. Bohjalian, C. *The Law of Similars*. New York: Vintage Press, 2000.
8. Jacobs, J., W. B. Jonas, M. Jimenez-Perez, and D. Crothers. "Homeopathy for Childhood Diarrhea: Combined Results and Meta-Analysis from Three Randomized, Controlled Clinical Trials." *Pediatric Infectious Disease Journal* 22, no. 3 (March 2003): 229–234.
9. Morrison, R. *Desktop Guide to Keynotes and Confirmatory Symptoms*. Nevada City, CA: Hahnemann Clinic Publishing, 1993, 305.
10. Website: aaaai.org/media/resources/media_kit/allergy_statistics.stm.

Chapter 11

1. Website: orthopedics.about.com/b/a/082678.htm.
2. Cell salts, or tissue salts, are homeopathic preparations made from some of the chemical elements found inside the cells of the human body—and also found elsewhere in nature. German physician Wilhelm Schuessler introduced them in 1873. He suggested the use of twelve preparations. Modern homeopathic companies sell fourteen. The two additional ones are combinations. Source is *The American Institute of Homeopathy Handbook for Parents* by E. Shalts. San Francisco, CA: Jossey-Bass, 2005.

Resources
Professional and Public Organizations

American Board of Homeotherapeutics (ABHt)
1913 Gladstone Drive
Wheaton, IL 60187
(630) 668-5595
homeopathyusa.org

American Institute of Homeopathy (AIH)
801 North Fairfax Street
Suite 306
Alexandria, VA 22314-1757
(888) 445-9988 (toll-free)
homeopathyusa.org

California Homeopathic Medical Society (CHMS)
169 East El Roblar Drive
Ojai, CA 93023
(805) 646-1495
homeopathywest.org

Council for Homeopathic Certification (CHC)
PMB 187
17051 Southeast 272nd Street
Suite 43
Covington, WA 98042
(866) 242-3399 (toll-free)
homeopathicdirectory.com

Council on Homeopathic Education (CHE)
91 Cornell Street
Newton, MA 02462-1320
(617) 244-8780
chedu.org

Florida Homeopathic Medical Society
668 Lake Villas Drive
Altamonte Springs, FL 32701
(407) 628-9708
prswan@aol.com

**Homeopathic Medical Society of the State of New York
(HMSSNY)**
6250 Route 9
Rhinebeck, NY 12572
(845) 876-6323
homeopathicmd@earthlink.net

Homeopathic Nurses Association (HNA)
8403 Tahona Drive
Silver Spring, MD 20903
(301) 445-0611

Homœopathic Pharmacopœia Convention of the United States (HPCUS)
P.O. Box 2221
Southeastern, PA 19399-2221
(610) 783-0987
hpcus.com

Illinois Homeopathic Medical Association
400 East 22nd Street
Suite F
Lombard, IL 60148
(630) 792-9311

National Board of Homeopathic Examiners (NBHE)
6536 Stadium Drive
Suite L
Zephyrhills, FL 33542
(813) 782-2690
nbhe.org

National Center for Homeopathy (NCH)
801 North Fairfax Street
Suite 306
Alexandria, VA 22314
(703) 548-7790
homeopathic.org
Publisher of *Homeopathy Today*. Open to the general public for membership; anyone can attend the annual conferences.

Ohio State Homeopathic Medical Society (OSHMS)
5779 Wooster Pike
Medina, OH 44256
(330) 784-4493

Texas Society of Homeopathy (TSH)
4200 Westheimer
Suite 100
Houston, TX 77025
(713) 621-3184
txsoho.com

Index

proving, 18–20
similars, 16–18
single remedy, 21–22
Ruta graveolens (garden rue)
fractures and, 228
injury, trauma, and, 79–80,
84–85
wrist conditions and, 241

Sabadilla (cevadilla seed), 208–9,
210, 213
Safety, 29–31
St. Anthony's turnip. See *Ranunculus
bulbosus*
St. Ignatius's bean, 137. See also
Ignatia amara
Saint-John's-wort. See *Hypericum
perforatum*
Salt. See *Natrum muriaticum*
Sanguinaria canadensis (bloodroot)
right-sided headaches and, 152–53,
154
shoulder pain and, 80, 84–85
vomiting and, 202–3, 205
Sarsaparilla, 221
Scarlet fever, 96, 107
Schuessler, Wilhelm, 26
Screaming babies, 118–19
Seasickness, 198, 203, 206, 235
Secale cornutum, 229
Selfridge, Grant L., 207
Sepia (cuttlefish ink)
left-sided headaches and, 154–56
nausea and vomiting and, 202–3,
206
Seven remedies, xv
Seven remedies, general descriptions
of
Aconitum, 51–54
Arnica, 71–75
Belladonna, 93–97
Chamomilla, 115–118
Gelsemium, 135–39

Ignatia, 157–62
Nux vomica, 175–80
Shakespeare, William, 157
Shalts, Edward, 253–54
Sharma, Vijay P., 178
Shingles (herpes zoster), 231–32
Shroyens, F., 45
Silica (silicon dioxide), 129, 132–33
Silicea, 33
Silver nitrate. See *Argentum
nitricum*
Similars, principle of, 16–18
SinEcch, 81, 221
Single remedy, principle of, 21–22
Sinusitis, 237–38
Snake bites, 87–90, 220
Sodium chloride. See *Natrum
muriaticum*
Sore throat
Belladonna for, 106–7, 112–13
other remedies for, 110–11
remedy comparison chart, 112–13
Spider veins, 241
Spiders, bites from, 87–90
Spigelia (pinkroot), 154–55, 156
Spinal injury, 79, 239
Spongia tosta (toasted sponge),
63–64, 224–25
Sprains and strains, 239–40
Stage fright, 139, 142, 240
Staphysagria, 84
Stinging nettle. See *Urtica urens*
Stramonium
nightmares and, 114, 235–36
post-traumatic stress and, 67
raw material of, 95
Strength-dilution paradox, 26
Succussion, 26
Suicidal depression, 168
Sulphur (brimstone)
diarrhea and, 188–89, 191
hemorrhoids and, 196–97
Sulphuricum acidum, 222

About the Author

EDWARD SHALTS, M.D., D.Ht., is trustee of the American Institute of Homeopathy and vice president of the National Center for Homeopathy. Born and raised in Russia, he graduated from medical school in Moscow. He practiced family medicine and homeopathy there until 1988, when he immigrated to the United States. For four years following his arrival, Dr. Shalts worked as a postdoctoral research scientist at Columbia University. He then completed psychiatric residency training at the Beth Israel Medical Center in New York City, where he served as chief resident. Afterward, he practiced homeopathy, conducted research, and taught for four years at the Continuum Center for Health and Healing, one of the largest centers of complementary and alternative medicine in the world, which is affiliated with the Beth Israel Medical Center. Currently, Dr. Shalts remains on the center's faculty and also has a private practice in New York City.

Dr. Shalts teaches a course in homeopathy for the alternative medicine curriculum of the New York College of Osteopathic Medicine and of the University of Medicine and Dentistry of New Jersey. He is a diplomate both of the American Board of Homeotherapeutics and of the American Board of Psychiatry and Neurology, and he is a founding diplomate of the American Board of Holistic Medicine. His office is located on the Upper West Side of Manhattan: Museum West Medical, 123 West 79th Street, Suite PH4, New York, NY 10024. Contact him by telephone, (212) 362-1884, or visit his website, homeopathynewyork.com.